Advance Praise

"David's ability to challenge your thinking and open your mind to other perspectives is unparalleled. David has such a talent to make you a better leader."

—JENN WEBB, GENERAL MANAGER, LINCOLN PLACE

"I am grateful for the opportunity to work with David and take advantage of his knowledge and expertise. David provided me with the coaching, tools, and encouragement I needed to help me get out of my comfort zone and grow as a manager and leader."

—SCOTT LANE, SENIOR DIRECTOR OF
STRATEGIC SOURCING, AIMCO

"David has a genuine desire to help his students objectively reflect and assess the important goals they want to achieve both professionally and personally. David guides you to focus on the things that really matter."

—ROSEMARIE HARRIS, PRINCIPAL, SECURED
SYSTEMS CONSULTING LLC

"Beyond the immediately applicable teachings and professional skills David brings to the table, his unique style of encouragement aided me in the discovery of what my true strengths and passions were, and his guidance helped me find real meaning in my work and life. I will forever be grateful for his impact, and I continue to credit his personal coaching with each and every success I achieve."

—CAROLYN DARLING, PROGRAM OFFICER, UNHCR; PROJECT MANAGER, COALITION OF HOPE

"David strikes the fine balance of the best coaches—just the right blend of challenge, encouragement, inspiration, and honesty. I'm a better leader today because of the time I spent with him."

—MATT HOLMES, SENIOR DIRECTOR OF PROCESS EXCELLENCE, AIMCO

"David is a fantastic trainer on all levels—energetic and passionate on all topics. I was genuinely inspired to look into myself and use the tools provided to help me achieve more in business and in everyday life."

—SANDRA HAYES, COMMUNITY MANAGER, ROYAL CREST ESTATES NASHUA

"David took the time to go over each lesson and explain when needed while also allowing a learning experience to naturally occur. David also provided a completely unbiased view and opinion when taking the teachings and applying them to real-world scenarios. It was a breath of fresh air to be taught and challenged at the same time."

—MATTHEW KINGHORN, GENERAL MANAGER, 21 FITZSIMONS

"David gave me tools to grow, take charge of my personal and professional life, manage my time more effectively, and feel reinvigorated as a leader."

—MARY BINIAK, ACCOUNTING DIRECTOR, AIMCO

"David Aduddell takes training to a different level. He asks the hard questions and digs deep, which allows the information to resonate with you. His approach reassures you that he is in this alongside you."

—CHARISE BENNETT, COMMUNITY MANAGER, MALIBU CANYON APARTMENTS

"David is a phenomenal leadership coach! I was able to look deeper inside myself and identify what was holding me back. Once identified, we created a plan with reachable goals to make personal improvements, which made a lasting impact on my career."

—SADLER WALKER, DIRECTOR ASSET MANAGEMENT, CARROLL ORGANIZATION

Breaking the Coaching Code

Breaking *the* Coaching Code

UNLOCKING THE FULL
POTENTIAL WITHIN YOURSELF
AND OTHERS

DAVID ADUDDELL

LIONCREST

PUBLISHING

BREAKING THE COACHING CODE

Unlocking the Full Potential Within Yourself and Others

ISBN   978-1-61961-767-4 *Paperback*

978-1-61961-768-1 *Ebook*

To Stephanie,

for all the contributions you made to this book, and more importantly, the contributions you have made to my life. You are the coach I aspire to one day become.

Contents

Foreword 13

PART I: THE COACHING CODE

Introduction 21
1. The Greatest Competitive Advantage 31
2. Tornado Alley 49
3. The New Rules of Coaching 69
4. Five Truths About Coaching...........................85

PART II: FEEDBACK

5. Introduction to Zone 1: Feedback 97
6. The SEEE Feedback Model 109
7. Feedback Mistakes to Avoid.......................... 117

PART III: TRAINING

8. Introduction to Zone 2: Training 137
9. MOR: A Better Way to Train 155

PART IV: MENTORING

10. Introduction to Zone 3: Mentoring.................175
11. Mentorship Agreements..............................187
12. Seven Traits of an Effective Mentor................ 199

PART V: COLLABORATION

13. Introduction to Zone 4: Collaboration 213
14. The RED Zone Collaboration Process.............. 235

PART VI: BREAKING THE COACHING CODE

15. Optimized Coaching.................................. 281
16. MAPS...289
17. The Coach's Playbook 329
Conclusion 375
Acknowledgments 385
About the Author....................................... 389

Foreword

BY ERIK PALMER

There is a Picasso Museum in Málaga, the city where Pablo Picasso was born. I had a chance to visit it when my wife and I spent some time touring Spain. When most people think of Picasso, they think of his Cubist period. They envision a triangle with one upside down eyeball inside the triangle, one eyeball outside of the triangle, and a title such as *Portrait of a Young Woman*. But long before Picasso developed Cubism, he mastered all aspects of painting. As a teenager, he was painting portraits and still lifes with photographic accuracy. He had sketchbooks filled with remarkable pencil and chalk drawings. And I was struck by how many of his works could convey a lot with only one or two lines. With one line, he revealed the posture of someone bending down; with a couple of lines, the flow of a woman's hair. There is genius in inventing a new style of painting, but there is also genius in being able to make the complex simple.

Breaking the Coaching Code demonstrates the second kind of genius. Coaching effectively is not an easy thing to do, and there are hundreds of books about the topic. As David Aduddell describes the vortex that consumes us at work, you'll recognize the vortex problem, and you'll realize that because of it, you don't have time to examine all the coaching resources out there. What if you could find one resource that synthesizes the key elements from the mass of material out there and makes the best ideas easily available? Aduddell has made that resource. A serious student of coaching, he has sifted through the best of what has been said and written, and he shares the gems of coaching advice with us. Peter Drucker, Albert Einstein, Malcolm Gladwell, Stephen Covey, and Mother Theresa, among others, all contribute. Powerful, on-point quotes are sprinkled throughout the book to reinforce the importance of the ideas presented.

But it's clear that Aduddell is not just sharing the best of others' work. He has been there. Twenty years of coaching has given him plenty of exposure to all the issues that businesses grapple with. Real-life examples from real workplaces are used, enabling us to see problems and solutions in action. You will recognize Jen and Latoya and Shane and Mario and many others. Looking at the mistakes they made (mistakes that many of us have made!) and seeing Aduddell's suggestions for avoiding and/or correcting them takes theory and puts it into practice. It isn't all business. Somehow his son mowing the lawn and a seventy-five-year-old man beating him at tennis provide insights also. Sharing his failures as well as his successes gives us assurance that we can all become effective coaches.

Clearly written, there are many moments of "Oh, I get it now!" Four kinds or "zones" of coaching and when to use each one? Five ways to give feedback, a model for how to give effective feedback, and mistakes to avoid? Pros and cons of various training methods and a method for setting up can't-miss trainings? Seven essentials for mentoring and seven traits of effective mentors? The two types of collaboration? Simple, understandable, and most importantly, doable. You'll recognize some of the ideas: Aduddell didn't invent SMART goals, but now you'll get a better picture of how and when to use them. He did invent MAPS, a brilliant way to set "the stage for better coaching." I get it.

In addition to the big ideas, the book is full of numerous strategies, small adjustments that can be easily made, and important questions to answer. It hadn't occurred to me the important difference between asking "What else?" and "Anything else?" The first implies there is more while the second allows for "Nope." Thinking of the "coachee" as an acorn instead of a vessel leads to a powerful change in thinking. And realizing how our stories—the notions we have concocted about situations and assume to be true—influence our views of reality can lead us to better understanding. Questions for reflection give us an opportunity to digest the ideas, and most importantly, the chapter titled "The Coach's Playbook" gives step-by-step questions to answer in order to prepare for the real game of coaching.

Think about March Madness, the tournament that wraps up the college basketball season. While there are always surprises, some coaches always seem to have their teams involved. Some coaches seem to be master coaches, better than the others. Maybe they are better at teaching players key skills, maybe they are better motivators, maybe they are better at finding and recruiting talent, or if you are cynical, maybe they are better at finding boosters to pay players and their families. For whatever reason, they are consistently at the top of the coaching game. I finished this book believing that I could be a top coach too.

If your workplace functions smoothly and is consistently high-functioning, this book isn't for you. Unfortunately, that kind of environment is rare. But it is achievable. Aduddell suggests that helping "individuals, leaders, and organizations create the culture that maximizes people first" is the way forward. *Breaking the Coaching Code* is full of practical ideas you can implement today to create the culture you want with successful, committed people around you. You can be the coach that positively transforms your company into a place where you and your coworkers will thrive.

—Erik Palmer, March 2018

Erik Palmer is a consultant, speaker, author, and conference presenter who specializes in helping others become confident, competent communicators. His books include Well Spoken, Digitally Speaking, Teaching the Core Skills of Listening & Speaking, Researching in a Digital World, Good Thinking, *and* Own Any Occasion.

Part I

THE COACHING
CODE

Introduction

LEFT BEHIND

Culture eats strategy for breakfast.

—PETER DRUCKER[1]

"I'm free!"

As those words echoed down the hallway, people stopped what they were doing and rolled their chairs out of their offices to get a peek at the source of the commotion. Who was yelling at the top of her lungs in the middle of the day at work? It was a woman—a disheveled woman in a business suit with a slightly crazed smile on her face. She tossed a folder full of papers into the air, and they bounced off the fluorescent lamps and fell to the carpeted floor.

---

1   Torben Rick, "Organizational Culture Eats Strategy for Breakfast, Lunch and Dinner," *Torben Rick*, June 11, 2014, accessed October 16, 2017, https://www.torbenrick.eu/blog/culture/organisational-culture-eats-strategy-for-breakfast-lunch-and-dinner.

Whispers: "Who is that?" "I think it's Jen." "Jen, who's Jen?" "You know...*Jen*."

Jen walked out of the building, and her coworkers rolled back into their offices and went back to work.

When I first met Jen, she was the shining star of the organization. We all looked up to her and wanted to be like her. Jen was invited to speak at company meetings and events, where management would whisper, "If only all our people could be like Jen." She was that kind of employee—a rising star destined to be the next company VP. They were grooming her for the role.

Jen was a director, and her team produced results. She'd had some big wins early on in her career and needed to keep winning to live up to her reputation. But while everyone outside her department saw her successes, no one imagined the whirlwind Jen was experiencing. Behind the scenes, she wasn't taking care of herself, getting enough sleep, or eating right. She had put on weight, her marriage was falling apart, and her kids felt like they were growing up without a mom.

Her team felt it too. They were starting to crack under the pressure of trying to meet Jen's expectations and demands, and one by one, they left the department. Jen's iconic reign began to crumble, and her solution was to pin the blame on something or someone else. She blamed everything: the market, the timing, and the pricing. She blamed her staff and the fact that she felt she was understaffed. But Jen had been riding on the success of her team, and as she drove them away, her numbers dropped fast.

One day, Jen got pulled into an office and was told she wasn't a cultural fit for the company anymore. As her numbers dropped and her people left, so did the company's passion for who she had been, who she still was, and who she might become. So they let her go, or more accurately, they got rid of her. The company sent Jen packing, and we all watched her walk out the door in a flurry of paperwork. Yet watching Jen leave like that—not with a whimper but a scream—wasn't the most unsettling part of her firing.

What disturbed me the most about Jen leaving the company was that everyone went back to what they were doing, and few ever spoke of Jen again.

THE CORPORATE VORTEX

Jen's demise within the organization is where my story begins. Her screams in that hallway that day awoke something inside of me that would shape my future as a coach. I made the commitment that I would no longer sit idly by and watch another individual with exceptional talent and potential fall into what I call the "corporate vortex."

The corporate vortex is a state of dysfunction that occurs when individuals and teams are consumed by unnecessary activities and misplaced priorities, and are unable to pursue intentional actions that provide meaningful results. The resulting dysfunction affects not only their work but can also alter their behavior, career satisfaction, and even their physical and emotional health. The vortex grows, creating further dysfunction throughout the organization, and often seeps into each person's personal life.

Too often, team members spend their days on activities that deplete their time and energy but produce meager advancements in performance or results. The assumption is that because they are *busy*—holding meetings, participating in conference calls, responding to emails, reading and building reports, holding team members accountable, trying to backfill positions, and looking for cost efficiencies (to name a few)—they are driving results.

In my work as a consultant, I worked closely with many very busy individuals to evaluate how much of their day was spent on impactful work, and the reality was alarming. In many cases, leaders indicated that 80 to 90 percent of their time was spent on activities that didn't drive results at all. In many cases, these leaders managed people on the same treadmill of inefficiency.

Over time, this corporate vortex drains the passion from people's roles. Their teams become fatigued and frustrated, working longer hours yet being less productive than they once were. The longer someone remains in the vortex, the higher the odds they will become discontent, apathetic, and ultimately, disengaged.

I discovered two measurements that help identify if an individual and an organization are stuck in the vortex, and they're correlated: (1) employee engagement and (2) retention. As engagement goes up, so does retention; when engagement suffers, turnover thrives. The corporate vortex shows up in metrics like customer satisfaction scores as well. When the vortex becomes a normal part of a company culture, destructive behaviors set in.

Symptoms of the vortex include silos between departments, knowledge brokering, politics and spin techniques, power struggles, constant fear and shaming, gossip, cliques, passive-aggressive behaviors, and the feeling of isolation and being on the outside. Every company has elements of these behaviors that show up from time to time; however, once they become a normal part of the culture, the vortex has taken over.

LIFE BEYOND THE VORTEX

How do you move past the vortex? The first step is to acknowledge the problem. Unfortunately, many leaders stuck in the vortex fail to realize it until much damage has been done.

Even now, as you are reading this introduction, you may be saying to yourself, "I am not a perfect leader, but I just need to hold things together a little longer. Things will get better after," and you fill in the blank with whatever is currently consuming your time, knowing that as soon as that project ends another one will show up to take its place. It's a faulty assumption that things will get better if you just keep going, because if you keep doing what you've always done, you'll keep getting what you've always gotten.

That's what happened to Jen. She kept driving her team and driving that vortex, thinking it would lift her to success, but instead, it swept her up and suffocated her. If Jen had stepped away from what she was doing and allowed herself a moment of clarity, she might have been able to recover. Instead, she drove herself to a place where she would either quit or get fired. Jen's numbers dropped, and when she stopped getting results, she didn't think about how she could change herself. Instead, like many senior leaders, she looked outside herself for a solution. If only she had better resources, a better staff, and better leadership, things would be different. If only she worked for a different company, she could be a tremendous success and a shining star—someplace else.

The fact is, it's hard to have an honest perspective of yourself when you're in the middle of a situation. That's why, for some, it's almost second nature to blame everything and everyone else when problems show up. There are many companies caught up in the corporate vortex, and their toxicity levels are through the roof. It's hard to get and stay healthy in a place like that. But usually, almost always, that toxic environment is affected by us—by you and me—and our behaviors. It is in those behaviors that you can destroy your results, your team, and yourself. It is also in those behaviors that you can propel yourself forward to tremendous success.

Jen failed herself by not taking responsibility for her actions (and reactions) and not taking steps to save herself, her team, and her job, but the company failed her too. They saw a problem—instead of a person—and got rid of it. They ignored their own contributions to Jen's fall from grace and took the easy way out, but at what cost? Aside from the moral implications, the financial impact of replacing someone—rather than identifying and correcting an issue—is perhaps much greater than people realize. The true cost of losing an employee or a team member is hard to quantify, but it's probably not a stretch to assume the cost is much higher than that person's annual salary. The immediate lost business coupled with the added cost of recruiting a new employee, training them, and allowing them time to ramp up to an acceptable level of competency is quite high.

The churn-and-burn mindset doesn't make moral or financial sense, and the emotional effects on other people in the organization who witness the upheaval may not be quantifiable. This doesn't mean a company should ignore bad behavior or underperformance. It does mean there is a better way to develop people so they operate at peak performance. The typical sink-or-swim management philosophy fails to equip high potential individuals with the resources necessary to ignite the brilliance within them, and not brilliance that's hidden deep down but often at the surface just waiting to be tapped.

One minor change to Jen's work situation would have prevented her from being sucked into the vortex. She didn't need any of the massive changes she thought she needed—like a new team or a new job—to get back on track. The company didn't need to get rid of her to fix the problem either. Jen failed, and her company failed her, but things could have turned out very differently for everyone if the company had a coaching culture and had—not as a matter of correction, but as a matter of course—provided Jen with a coach.

BREAKING THE COACHING CODE

The last thing you probably need right now is more to do, and doing more isn't necessary anyway. This book isn't about overhauling your organization. Instead, I'm going to show you how, through coaching, you can do a few things differently to drastically change your performance and results. By using the principles and tools provided in the following pages, you will be able to move past the corporate vortex holding you hostage so you can create an authentic and productive culture. For those trapped in a cycle of constant activities that seem to be leading you nowhere, you will learn how to shift to meaningful behaviors that produce measurable results.

You deserve a better workplace, a better environment, a healthier culture, and more positive results. You deserve it, and you have everything you need to make it happen. I'm going to show you how to use what you already have, to change the way you approach the people in your life—your coworkers, leaders, internal customers, and the people who work for you. We're going to help Jen, and we're going to help ourselves because Jen's life and career are no way to live and work. There's a better way, a simpler way, to succeed, and without sacrificing what's most important—yourself.

Breaking the Coaching Code is designed to help individuals, leaders, and organizations create the culture that maximizes people first. Take care of your people first, and you will see far greater results. In the chapters ahead, I will show you how to make small shifts in your organization's behaviors from the inside out. These small shifts have the power to produce giant leaps in creating highly effective cultures and positive change. By unlocking the potential within your team, you will transform your performance and ultimately achieve maximum results.

CHAPTER 1

The Greatest Competitive Advantage

Behind every fearless player is a fearless coach who refused to let them be anything but the best they can be.

—ANONYMOUS

Several years ago, I came across an article about the difference between the top and bottom professional golfers. The author claimed the difference between the number-one player and last-place player is often less than three strokes average over the course of a season.[1] If you think about it, that's remarkable. The best golfer in the world is better, but not by much. The competition is extreme, fighting to move up in that small gap between the best and the worst. How

---

1   Austin Vickers, "The Difference Between Good and Great," *People v. the State of Illusion*, October 21, 2012, accessed October 16, 2017, http://thestateofillusion.com/2012/10/the-difference-between-good-and-great.

do these athletes give themselves a competitive advantage when the margins are so tight? When every stroke counts, how do they know how to get more from their shots, and more importantly, more from themselves?

This is when I realized the best of the best have coaches. It doesn't matter what sport or industry, the top performers usually have someone outside of themselves providing direction and guidance to help them improve their performance. These individuals don't rely solely on talent and willpower. They have someone to tell them not what they want to hear but what they need to hear. When others give up and go home, these people have a coach who pushes them to keep going. The same is true for exceptional leaders. Extraordinary leaders don't get into top positions because of their educational credentials or their IQ scores. Top leaders—the ones driving healthy innovation and change—have coaches. Coaching is the greatest competitive advantage for anyone looking to be the best of the best.

AVOIDING SILVER BULLETS

Over the last twenty years, I have worked with organizations and companies to find ways to improve efficiencies, performance, and bottom-line results. Inevitably, at any organization, there are leaders looking for a silver bullet that will solve their problems and grow their business. These leaders pore over the latest business books and articles looking for the newest trends and success formulas. They hire outside consultants, coaches, and trainers to come in and provide a formula to magically make their problems disappear while increasing their dividends for stakeholders. Who could blame them for wanting to find that one unicorn idea or process that would turn their entire organization into a world-class leader? We hear about these miracle moments that some companies experience and wonder how to replicate them. For example, when a simple phone app becomes the biggest sensation of the year, people take notice and want to know what they can do to achieve that same kind of overnight success. Ever hear of Pokémon Go or Candy Crush?

Unfortunately, the odds of finding a silver bullet that solves all your organizational gaps are about the same as winning the Powerball lottery (and the Powerball odds are about one in 292 million, according to Google). Think about all the company initiatives you have been a part of over the years in your career. From fad trainings to flavor-of-the-month programs, many of these initiatives fail before they even begin. Consider the wasted time, energy, and money spent on ineffective programs with little to no return on your investment.

The good news is there are initiatives that stick and that can help you reap lucrative returns. They transform the culture and drive health within the organization. These programs can provide a huge advantage in this highly competitive economy. Many of these programs have common traits. As the great business coach Tony Robbins puts it, "Success leaves clues."

INSIDE-OUT SOLUTIONS WORK BEST

Authentic and impactful change often begins on the inside. People are more passionate and committed to their own ideas than they are to those introduced by an outsider telling them how to think and act, or by an outside program that will magically solve their work woes. I believe the primary role of leaders and managers, along with external consultants, coaches, and trainers, is to help organizations bring out the best in their own people. Too often, I have seen outside support become an attempt to bring in the brilliance. If leaders and talent management groups have done their part to hire good people, our greatest return on investment is to inspire and bring out the best in these individuals, and not inundate them with one-size-fits-all solutions that don't consider their unique business, situation, people, preferences, strengths, weaknesses, skills, and needs. I uncovered this clue early on in my consulting career and, since then, have seen inside-out solutions transform teams on many occasions.

For example, I was recently hired to work with a team of senior leaders struggling to communicate effectively together. When one of the leaders of the organization first reached out for my help, he wanted me to come in and somehow fix his people. The assumption for this leader, as is with many organizations, is that the people were somehow broken. After meeting with the team, I didn't see broken people. However, I could tell their communication methods were not working effectively any longer. Keep in mind, our behaviors and processes work until they don't. Then we must explore new ways of addressing issues. For this team, I used a behavioral assessment to help them learn some additional tools to understand themselves and each other better. The result was not that I fixed them or their communication. Rather, I created an environment for them to fix themselves. They came up with ideas and methods that were far superior to my bag of tricks. I didn't have to sell them on my ideas. They bought in and committed to their solutions right away.

The most exciting part for me—and an obvious clue that inside-out solutions are often more successful—was watching these people suddenly feel empowered to solve their own problems.

MAXIMIZING TOP TALENT

The next clue I discovered, consulting with businesses that struggled and those that succeeded, was the power of maximizing top talent.

In this emerging economy, many business gurus cite two key components that organizations must have in place to gain a competitive edge: speed to market and innovation through technology. These components can accelerate your business in the race for market share, but their effects are short term and won't get you to the finish line. Having the right people in place to sustain and effectively run your infrastructure is a requirement for long-term high performance and growth.

A blended approach of all three key components—people, technology, and speed—is necessary to accelerate growth, and, of the three, an investment in people is first and foremost. Over the next five to ten years, an organization's single greatest competitive advantage will be their ability to attract, develop, and retain top talent. Hiring the right people, developing them to their full potential through coaching, and getting them to stay will have a dramatic impact on productivity, and the long-term effects of optimized productivity on return on investment cannot be overstated. In fact, the great business guru Peter Drucker hypothesized that, if an organization increases employee productivity by 10 percent, the organization will double its profits.[2]

Let that sink in for a moment. Without spending any additional dollars on marketing, advertising, customer service, sales, or production, an organization can double its profits by leveraging people more effectively for greater productivity.

---

2   John H. Zenger and Kathleen Stinnett, *The Extraordinary Coach: How the Best Leaders Help Others Grow* (New York: McGraw-Hill, 2010), 3.

Imagine the potential for increased profits for a company that can attract, develop, and retain top talent—the best internal customers—and then leverage and optimize those internal customers' skills.

Still, too many companies rely on the churn-and-burn method of workforce employment: hiring, firing, and simply losing good people because they do not value the potential their employees bring to the business. This philosophy has devastating consequences: high turnover, low engagement, limited institutional knowledge, and impaired creativity, to name just a few. Companies are learning the hard way that simply throwing money at the problem to attract high-caliber people isn't the solution either. Paying higher salaries or providing robust benefits does not compensate for a dysfunctional work environment.

There is, however, a simpler way to address engagement and turnover that's more beneficial for the company, that's more satisfying for the employee, and that achieves greater long-term results for everyone. While the science of employee retention is far more complicated than the scope of this book allows, five core elements have been found to directly affect attracting and retaining talent: performance, development, contribution, recognition, and fun.

Many companies have one or two of these elements integrated in their cultural behaviors, but organizations that have focused on all five have experienced lower turnover and increased employee engagement. Successful organizations have learned to incorporate each of these five elements into their culture in some way.

One example of this is Southwest Airlines. *Entrepreneur* magazine published an article titled "5 Companies Getting Employee Engagement Right" in which the airline was featured as a company revered for their employee engagement practices. Southwest isn't new to high-engagement scores; they have been leading in this space for years. From the article:

> With employee engagement levels having remained high over the years, they have a team full of committed, enthusiastic people who are passionate about the company's vision and values and willing to help the company continue their success.[3]

Southwest allowed their employees to design their own uniforms, giving them a say in a decision normally dictated by outside consultants or marketing firms. Employees used this freedom to express their personalities and that of the company's unique culture. Southwest Airlines's leaders promote creativity and innovation. From a viral video of a flight attendant rapping the safety announcement to the

---

3 Steffen Maier, "5 Companies Getting Employee Engagement Right," *Entrepreneur*, December 28, 2016, accessed October 12, 2017, https://www.entrepreneur.com/article/285052.

CEO giving weekly shout-outs to employees, this playful environment values people and connects them as individuals, and as a company. Southwest Airlines's competitors try to replicate what the airline has done, often by manufacturing an inauthentic environment and culture, but as Southwest's cofounder Herb Kelleher said, "They can buy all the physical things. The things you can't buy are dedication, devotion, loyalty—the feeling that you are participating in a crusade."

Southwest Airlines's employees are engaged because they have the freedom to have fun at work while contributing in creative, meaningful ways that affect the success of the organization. They are encouraged to develop and grow and are recognized for their achievements. These employee engagement practices are key to fostering employee talent and maximizing top talent.

Let's examine the five core elements in greater detail. Then we will explore how to incorporate them into your corporate culture in an authentic and powerful way.

PERFORMANCE

The first element is ensuring your employees feel their work matters to the business and impacts the bottom line. People must know they're competing for a reason, and they need a clear goal and a clear plan to achieve it. Their measure of success in meeting that goal must be clearly defined.

This is often not the case. For example, a sales organization conducted an internal survey in which their field employees were asked to rate their own performance compared to that of their peers. Sixty-four percent said they were in the top quartile of performers, 32 percent said they were in the top half, and just 3 percent believed they were in the bottom half. Only one person in the sales organization thought they were in the bottom quartile. This is a glaring example of what happens when winning is not clearly defined. It also indicates that performance expectations were inconsistent, and people were not being provided with ongoing coaching.

If, prior to this survey, you asked the leadership team if their people clearly understood what was expected of them, they would likely have said, "Of course." This was demonstrated by the fact that leaders scored themselves at 75 percent when asked if they had regular conversations with their team members to show support, direction, and guidance. However, when their subordinates were asked about these conversations, they scored these same leaders at 44 percent. This showed a disconnect where leaders assumed their people had a clear understanding of performance expectations. Also, it showed that leaders assume they are having better coaching moments with their people than they are.

DEVELOPMENT

Individuals must feel they are growing and developing. This

is not only a job requirement for fulfilling one of the five core elements of employee engagement; it is a human need. Unfortunately, many leaders equate growth with promotions. More often, people develop not with a change in title but by challenging themselves with fresh projects and situations that develop their mind and skills. Employees crave personal and professional growth, and organizations that create growth cultures benefit, too, because their people will often stay for less pay and a lower position if they feel they are continuously learning. Also, not everyone wants to climb the proverbial corporate ladder, but most want the opportunity to better themselves, especially if they can do so within their workplace and with the support of their leaders.

CONTRIBUTION

The third element is contribution. People want to feel their life, their time, and their organization are making the world a better place. Beyond hitting key performance indicators or landing large contracts, people want to feel their lives matter. They want to leave a legacy and show how their contribution played a role in shaping a change for the better. This is why so many organizations have adopted corporate volunteer programs, corporate matching initiatives, and paid hours that employees can use to give back to their favorite cause or charity.

Contribution is not only tied to external venues. Individuals also want to feel they are contributing to the success of the organization on the inside. For example, how leaders treat and interact with the maintenance staff, the frontline reps, or the front-desk receptionist has a direct correlation to how these individuals perceive their value. It is essential for leaders to understand that highly effective organizations see every role as contributing to the success of the company. They must work hard to help everyone understand how their piece of the process is critical to the success of the entire organization.

Employees who make direct contributions—such as the engineers, salespeople, and the IT department—are usually valued at a company, but consider those who are often overlooked. What would a day at your office be like if the cleaning people didn't show up to empty the trash, tidy up the breakroom, or clean out the refrigerators? How might that affect your day? What would it be like if the administrative assistant didn't come to work? Think about the work those people do and how it contributes to your experience at work and to your company's success.

RECOGNITION

Recognition can be promoted by leaders in many ways. When a leader provides consistent, authentic, and sincere recognition, they transform the way people perform. Their people work longer and harder. Petty differences seem to melt away as team members focus on core objectives, all because their leader took the time to acknowledge them. Recognition can be spontaneous or delivered as a regular, timely event. For example, a leader might end the day by getting out of their office to address the team face-to-face, calling out all the specific successes of the day and the people responsible. The leader could start the day with an email to the team, recounting the previous day's successes and how they supported the culture of the business or furthered the team's progress toward its goals. Recognition lets people know their efforts aren't being overlooked or taken for granted and can inspire others to work toward similar efforts.

FUN

Finally, the fifth core element of engaging employees and maximizing top talent is the incorporation of fun into the workplace. Playful activities allow individuals to express themselves. They open the door to laughter and refreshed perspectives.

Many companies take themselves too seriously. Like the proverb goes, "All work and no play make Jack a dull boy." All work and no play also make Jack want to work somewhere else. HR leaders, and others in management, point to the quarterly potluck or surprise birthday celebrations (that are neither a surprise nor fun) as proof of their fun culture. Many fear that a focus on fun would create a lax and unprofessional work environment, worrying that frivolity will take over and that people will fail to achieve their deliverables. Understand that people can only stay focused on one thing for so long, and people at work check out often, with or without your approval: catching up on Facebook, playing games on their phones, or texting friends and loved ones, all the while pretending to stare intently at their computer screen. These behaviors just aren't always visible to leaders, but leaders can accept their employees' need to break from the intensity of the workday to engage in moments of fun.

Author Jim Collins of *Good to Great* says, "Twenty percent of our success is the new technology that we embrace…[but] eighty percent of our success is in the culture of our company."[4] The question now is, how do you take steps to create this type of culture in your organization?

THE COACHING EVOLUTION

All these clues, and the five core components to employee engagement—retention, talent maximization, and productivity—are impacted by one powerful tool: coaching. Coaching can provide a shift in behaviors that impacts the culture—the soul—of an organization.

A paradigm shift doesn't happen through the introduction of

---

4   Jim Collins, *Good to Great: Why Some Companies Make the Leap and Others Don't* (New York: HarperCollins, 2001).

new tools and tactics; it happens when we shift our thinking and beliefs. This shift transforms performance, and ultimately, results. A proven, efficient, and effective method for affecting this shift is available to leaders through coaching.

WHERE DO YOU RATE?

Take a moment and think about your current work environment. Some companies do well in performance, but when it comes to fun, they are totally lost. In other organizations, people have a good time, but there is little or no recognition for achievement. You need a balance of all five components for a healthy, thriving culture, one that encourages people to stay and creates a competitive edge in the marketplace.

On a scale of one to ten, how does your company rate in these five areas?

1. **Performance**: My employees feel their work matters to the business and impacts the bottom line. _____

2. **Contribution**: My employees feel they, and the organization, are making the world a better place. _____

3. **Development**: My employees are continuously learning new skills through on-the-job training, formal coursework, or new projects that challenge their abilities and provide opportunities for personal and professional growth. _____

4. **Recognition**: My employees feel that their work is recognized and not overlooked or taken for granted. _____

5. **Fun**: My employees have opportunities to express themselves and have fun. _____

Moving forward, we don't need shiny new processes to make our problems go away. The best solutions are those that have worked historically and focus on people. We need to return to the fundamentals of how we treat people. Employees are not assets. We don't tag them like laptops. They are human beings with the power to propel a company forward—or derail an entire organization.

People—the right people in the right positions with the right organizational support—are the solution. Human resources works closely with leadership to attract and hire the right people for an organizational need. This can be a time- and resource-intensive process, but hiring the right candidate is so important that no one wants to get it wrong, and no one involved in that process has any incentive to do it poorly. Let's assume you are hiring the right people. That's the first part of the equation.

The second part of the equation is the ongoing coaching required to ensure those people whom you have taken great pains to identify and bring on as employees, don't become the wrong people for your organization. This is exactly what happens when you neglect the second part of the equation: coaching. Hiring gets you the right people, coaching keeps them the right people, and continuous coaching empowers them to become the people they need to be as the organization evolves and the needs of the company change.

This is only possible when coaching is recognized not as a corrective action but as an ongoing practice, which is critical to an employee's development and their subsequent, professional success and the success of the organization. When companies empower their employees through coaching to develop a culture of learning, the right people with the right attitudes and skills will naturally be there when you need them.

CHAPTER 2

Tornado Alley

People don't have time to do it right, but they do have time to do it wrong over and over again.

—PAT PARELLI

If coaching is key to optimizing personal and team performance, why is it usually done so poorly or overlooked completely? Why do leaders fail to take advantage of coaching to improve their teams and organizations? In many cases, leaders aren't even aware of the problems that arise and opportunities that are missed due to a lack of coaching. This oversight is due, in part, to the slow, steady, development of issues that grow, undetected, filling the coaching vacuum—a corporate vortex that grows over time.

I grew up in Oklahoma in the heart of tornado alley. As a child, I had my share of tornado drills at home and at school to prepare for a sudden storm that could arise and become dangerous very quickly. I can still imagine the wails of the tornado sirens, warning everyone to take cover immediately. Adrenaline would pulse through my body as I raced to the designated shelter area. Living in that part of the country, a tornado was something you grew to respect and fear. Over time, you could see the power and destruction these storms had on cars, homes, businesses, and ultimately, on the lives they touched. What amazed me the most about tornadoes was how quickly they could manifest themselves, cut a path of absolute carnage, and be gone within minutes.

As an adult, I have seen similar storms manifest themselves in work environments as corporate vortexes. As previously defined in the introduction, the corporate vortex is a state of dysfunction that occurs when individuals and teams are consumed by unnecessary activities and misplaced priorities, and are unable to pursue intentional actions that provide meaningful results. This dysfunction develops slowly but strikes suddenly, as productivity is replaced by activity. Individuals are swept up in a constant cyclone of busyness with little regard for effectiveness, creating an unhealthy environment for the people involved and for the organization as a business.

It's important to note that busyness and activity do not necessarily signal a corporate vortex. Busy offices full of constant activity can be very healthy environments. It is the dysfunction caused by a lack of intention and purpose—leading to actual productivity and desired outcomes—that differentiates the vortex from a typical, busy office environment.

In cultures where the corporate vortex is dominant, you will see a constant influx of symptoms. Common side effects include feeling overworked, underappreciated, long-term fatigue, frustration, constant fear, low creativity, high turnover, low engagement, increased blame and excuses, reduced productivity, minimal results, and even death of the company.

That sounds severe—like a dire warning on the side of a deadly prescription drug. In fact, left untreated, the vortex can be lethal to business. Companies can perish from a vortex that starts off as a little storm and quickly becomes their corporate culture. It destroys them from the inside out.

As a business seeking a competitive edge, your greatest opposition may not be the company down the street. Your greatest challenge may be hidden in your own office.

DISPERSING THE VORTEX: SHANE'S SITUATION

Vortexes may be found in any business or industry. I was once hired by a large car dealership that had a 40 percent turnover rate—mind you, this was 40 percent every quarter, not every year. This constant turnover was affecting company morale and customer interactions and destroying their bottom line. I spoke with the general manager and senior leaders, who told me their mantra was "We treat people like family around here." They said they went above and beyond to support their people. So why were so many of them leaving?

When I casually interviewed the people on the sales floor, I got a very different story. The word "family" didn't come up once. I did hear the words "fear," "frustration," and "communication problems." At management's request, I spoke privately with one salesperson. Management wanted me to coach Shane, but it was obvious they had already made up their minds to terminate him. They were going through the motions to cover their bases before giving him the boot. After speaking with Shane, I quickly realized the people who needed coaching—much more than the employees—were the leaders themselves.

Shane had been a rock star at the dealership, but his numbers were declining drastically. Management thought he had checked out and didn't want to be there anymore. Shane, on the other hand, had a very different story. He was working hard to keep up with the demands of the business. Specifically, he was struggling to balance his personal life as a single parent and the long hours of selling cars.

His leaders kept tacking on responsibilities and activities they thought would increase sales. These new initiatives forced salespeople to work longer hours, burning them out, and distracting them from their primary role of selling cars and servicing customers. Leaders felt their people were becoming disengaged and apathetic, and the pressure mounted. They thought they needed better salespeople, so they began firing employees. As people left, the shortage of competent employees added to the stress on those who remained, affecting customer satisfaction scores. This caused even more pressure for everyone. The vortex, unchecked, was affecting business and devastating the company culture.

Despite what his leaders believed, Shane was still a rock star, and he wanted to be there. They all did. The problem was in communication and a lack of coaching for the right reasons. As I partnered with the leaders and the sales team to discuss the true problems they were facing, the solution became apparent, and it was simple.

The company's management had to learn to communicate with employees and stop using coaching as a CYA (the proverbial "Cover Your Ass") process and see it, instead, as an educational, supportive, kind, and caring gesture. By making this one change, the team was able to stop the vortex before it destroyed their careers and the dealership.

A couple months later, I visited the dealership again. Shane had returned to being one of their top sales makers. More importantly, the employee turnover had dropped dramatically. People were excited to come to work again, and the changes in the culture were bringing positive results to their bottom line.

How do you know if your organization is in the vortex? It's not always obvious, especially if you don't know the symptoms. Let's take a moment to see if the corporate vortex is affecting your organization.

DETERMINE YOUR ORGANIZATION'S V-SCORE

The corporate vortex that creates and reinforces a communication chasm can be corrected, but the first step is identifying it. The following assessment is a simple, introductory exercise for determining your vortex score, or V-Score.

Take a few moments to read the questions, and then select your answers. There are no right or wrong choices; rather, the assessment's aim is to help you identify vortex symptoms around matters like engagement, turnover, spending, and productivity so you can better determine their likely sources.

From the twenty groups of statements below, select the statement that best reflects your work environment, with 1 representing the first statement (left) and 10 representing the second statement (right). You may select any number from 1 to 10 in the range.

1. ① ② ③ ④ ⑤ ⑥ ⑦ ⑧ ⑨ ⑩

My organization extends trust to others.

My organization is distrustful of others.

2. ① ② ③ ④ ⑤ ⑥ ⑦ ⑧ ⑨ ⑩

In my organization, sharing the truth will have a negative impact on my job.

In my organization, my opinions are welcomed and valued.

3. ① ② ③ ④ ⑤ ⑥ ⑦ ⑧ ⑨ ⑩

My company struggles to find strong candidates to hire.

My company leads in recruiting top talent.

4. ① ② ③ ④ ⑤ ⑥ ⑦ ⑧ ⑨ ⑩

My company operates in silos of mistrust.

We work collectively as one team.

5. ① ② ③ ④ ⑤ ⑥ ⑦ ⑧ ⑨ ⑩

My organization is disengaged or apathetic.

My organization is highly engaged and productive.

6. ① ② ③ ④ ⑤ ⑥ ⑦ ⑧ ⑨ ⑩

My company blames others for mistakes.

My company takes ownership for decisions no matter the outcome.

7. ① ② ③ ④ ⑤ ⑥ ⑦ ⑧ ⑨ ⑩

My company ignores employees and fails to provide feedback.

My company consistently develops employees and provides growth opportunities.

8. ① ② ③ ④ ⑤ ⑥ ⑦ ⑧ ⑨ ⑩

My company avoids taking risks.

My company fosters an environment of creativity and innovation.

9. ① ② ③ ④ ⑤ ⑥ ⑦ ⑧ ⑨ ⑩

My company spends money and resources on wasteful items.

My company leads in cost efficiencies.

10. ① ② ③ ④ ⑤ ⑥ ⑦ ⑧ ⑨ ⑩

My organization is constantly changing priorities and having fire drills.

My organization displays well-planned and unwavering program management.

11. ① ② ③ ④ ⑤ ⑥ ⑦ ⑧ ⑨ ⑩

The leadership at my company could be described as one of command and control.

The leadership at my company is collaborative and empowering.

12. ① ② ③ ④ ⑤ ⑥ ⑦ ⑧ ⑨ ⑩

My company follows industry trends.   My company innovates our industry.

13. ① ② ③ ④ ⑤ ⑥ ⑦ ⑧ ⑨ ⑩

At my company, everyone is out for themselves.

At my company, I trust my leaders and feel they have my best interest in mind when making decisions.

14. ① ② ③ ④ ⑤ ⑥ ⑦ ⑧ ⑨ ⑩

My company avoids or ignores difficult conversations.

My company confronts issues in a safe and healthy way.

15. ① ② ③ ④ ⑤ ⑥ ⑦ ⑧ ⑨ ⑩

I am uncertain where my organization is headed.

I am helping to shape the future of my company.

16. ① ② ③ ④ ⑤ ⑥ ⑦ ⑧ ⑨ ⑩

I am uncertain of success metrics.

I have clearly aligned performance indicators.

17. ① ② ③ ④ ⑤ ⑥ ⑦ ⑧ ⑨ ⑩

My company does whatever it takes to achieve goals, even if it violates company values.

My company is unwavering in its core values to maintain integrity.

18. ① ② ③ ④ ⑤ ⑥ ⑦ ⑧ ⑨ ⑩

My company takes credit for what others do.

My company consistently recognizes and rewards team members' efforts.

19. ① ② ③ ④ ⑤ ⑥ ⑦ ⑧ ⑨ ⑩

My company uses gossip and information to broker political gain.

My company fosters healthy communication and addresses issues appropriately.

20. ① ② ③ ④ ⑤ ⑥ ⑦ ⑧ ⑨ ⑩

The people at my company often talk about leaving for a better opportunity.

The people at my company are committed to the organization.

What did you discover about the vortex symptoms in your organization? Where do they lie? With your leadership? Your team? Although every organization struggles to deal with the vortex to some degree, many organizations experience greater effects from it. The vortex prevents them from experiencing their potential growth and prevents their people from getting the most out of their time and efforts. What could you achieve if the vortex wasn't dominating your company's culture? If you and your team were freed up to operate at your full capacity? How would things be different if you felt safe to fail and free to try innovative ideas? How much more would you give if you felt appreciated and valued?

Take a moment to review your responses to the V-Score Assessment. Then answer the following questions:

- Of the twenty groups of statements, where is your company excelling? List three areas where your company is free from the vortex.

1. ....

2. ....

3. ....

- Where are the vortex symptoms most prominently displayed? List three areas where there is the greatest opportunity for improvement.

1. ....

2. ....

3. ....

THE PATH TO CHANGE: DAVID'S DILEMMA

Men do not attract that which they want, but that which they are.

—JAMES ALLEN, AS A MAN THINKETH

After identifying the corporate vortex within an organization, taking steps to affect change may seem daunting. Some leaders take the assessment, identify several areas of concern, but feel powerless to correct them. They feel their only option is to accept the problems, dismissing them with trite phrases such as, "It is what it is." In other words, they choose to accept the situation because they believe they are unable to influence or control it. But is this a reality?

I learned the answer to this question the hard way. As the senior leader over a team of about one hundred people, I was surprised when one of my peers was promoted to a higher position. He and I had, at one time, worked closely together, so reporting to him was awkward for both of us. He didn't know how to manage me, and I didn't want to be managed by him.

At the time, I was one of the highest performers in the region, but I got caught in the corporate vortex. Frustrated over my situation, I blamed everyone and everything, and my attitude affected my productivity. My numbers dropped, and instead of taking responsibility or reaching out to my coach for direction and support, I pointed my finger at my new leader. I was certain my failure was his fault, and when I badmouthed him behind his back, my coworkers agreed with me. We talked about what a terrible leader he was and how he was hurting our numbers by not supporting us properly. Around this same time, my department began experiencing

HR and staffing issues, and it was easy for me to blame these problems on my new leader.

My failing numbers and poor attitude caused our relationship to disintegrate. Convinced I'd soon be fired whenever that leader came to town, I cleaned out my company vehicle and prepared for the worst. Then, I did what all "great" leaders do when they think they're not being appreciated—I went online to look for another job. This was my lowest point in a corporate vortex, but I had to hit rock bottom before I could open my eyes to the truth of the situation and my responsibility in it.

One day, I was venting to my coach about my situation when he asked, "David, have you ever considered the problem might not be your leader?"

"Have you not been listening to me?" I asked. "These decisions, these problems, and this lack of support are all because of him."

"I'm not telling you what to do," he said, "but you might look to see whether there's someone else at fault."

Hmmm...I couldn't imagine who he might be talking about. Surely, these problems had nothing to do with me! It wasn't long before my boss came back to town. I decided it was time to tell him about my concerns.

"I can't do this anymore," I told him.

"You can't do what?" he asked.

"All of this. I feel you don't like me, and you don't respect me. I feel you would prefer to not have me on your team. If you want my resignation, you can have it today because I can't keep this up."

He looked at me and said, "You know, it's funny you should say that because I feel the same, that you don't like or respect me and don't want to work for me."

In that moment I realized my problem wasn't sitting next to me in the car, it was facing me in the mirror. I was the problem. I'd been projecting all my fears, insecurities, and shortcomings onto this leader when I was the one failing to live up to my abilities and aspirations. With him as my scapegoat, I didn't have to accept responsibility for my situation.

After that conversation, I stopped blaming him. I accepted responsibility and took control of my situation. I apologized to the man for badmouthing him to my peers and undermining him with my own failure. From that day on, he and I built a new relationship on honesty, trust, and personal responsibility. I pulled myself out of the corporate vortex, and within a month, my numbers went to the top. All the staffing issues were resolved, and the HR problems went away. My people, sensing the change in me, started dealing with their own issues in a healthier way too. Eventually, that leader gave me an additional market to manage, and I continued to experience remarkable success running the two top markets in the area for our company.

These positive changes didn't occur by hiring a new team, getting a new boss, or taking a new direction with my work. Rather, I became a different person, and my results changed with me. Thriving in the corporate vortex didn't require fixing my team, my leader, or my organization—or jumping ship to join a new one. Fixing myself made the difference, and it took a coach to open my eyes to the reality of my situation. Accepting responsibility instead of blaming someone else for my problem empowered me to become the person I needed to be, and to create an environment where my team could be who they needed to be. Sometimes even coaching experts need coaches to help them be their very best.

Thriving in the corporate vortex doesn't demand an epiphany. You can make better choices for yourself, your team, and your organization every day, starting today. You have more control and ability to survive whatever storm you're in than you realize. Think of yourself as a boat at sea. Caught up in a storm, you can fight the waves and get tossed about, or you can adjust your sails and rudder and navigate the waters. There will always be storms, and vortexes will always exist to some extent, but it is within you to adjust and survive them. All you need is a little direction. When you feel like you're adrift at sea or being tossed by the waves, a coach can be the beacon who guides you toward smooth sailing and a brighter horizon.

YOUR ROLE IN THE VORTEX

Before you can be a great coach for others, you must be accountable for your own success and happiness. Only then will you be in a position and proper frame of mind to help others be accountable for themselves. This accountability begins with awareness.

John Whitmore, author of *Coaching for Performance*, put it this way: "I am able to control only that of which I am aware. That of which I am unaware controls me. Awareness empowers me."[1]

Inspired by this powerful concept, I paraphrased his words, and they have become my own personal mantra:

THE THINGS I AM AWARE OF, I CAN CONTROL. THE THINGS I AM UNAWARE OF CONTROL ME.

---

[1]   John Whitmore, Coaching for Performance: GROWing Human Potential and Purpose: The Principles and Practice of Coaching and Leadership, 4th ed. (Boston: Nicholas Brealey, 2009).

YOUR V-SCORE: A DETAILED ASSESSMENT

You evaluated your company. Now it's time to evaluate your personal role in the vortex. Only then can you move on to the next steps, learning new tools and their application for solving problems within your control. To complete the vortex self-assessment, read the following twenty statements. Then, circle the number below each to indicate your agreement or disagreement with the statement, with 1 being totally disagree and 10 being completely agree.

MY TEAM:

1. My team looks for ways to go above and beyond in all we do.

① ② ③ ④ ⑤ ⑥ ⑦ ⑧ ⑨ ⑩

2. My team is a good steward of our time and resources.

① ② ③ ④ ⑤ ⑥ ⑦ ⑧ ⑨ ⑩

3. My team is passionate in all they do.

① ② ③ ④ ⑤ ⑥ ⑦ ⑧ ⑨ ⑩

4. My team feels valued and appreciated.

① ② ③ ④ ⑤ ⑥ ⑦ ⑧ ⑨ ⑩

5. My team consistently works at their full potential.

① ② ③ ④ ⑤ ⑥ ⑦ ⑧ ⑨ ⑩

6. My team clearly knows what winning is for our organization.

① ② ③ ④ ⑤ ⑥ ⑦ ⑧ ⑨ ⑩

7. My team can always count on me to do what I say I am going to do.

① ② ③ ④ ⑤ ⑥ ⑦ ⑧ ⑨ ⑩

8. I am my team's biggest fan.

① ② ③ ④ ⑤ ⑥ ⑦ ⑧ ⑨ ⑩

9. My team knows I will be there to support them if they make a mistake.

① ② ③ ④ ⑤ ⑥ ⑦ ⑧ ⑨ ⑩

10. My team would say I am a highly effective leader.

① ② ③ ④ ⑤ ⑥ ⑦ ⑧ ⑨ ⑩

MYSELF:

1. I attract and retain top talent.

① ② ③ ④ ⑤ ⑥ ⑦ ⑧ ⑨ ⑩

2. I have a clear plan of where we are going as a team.

① ② ③ ④ ⑤ ⑥ ⑦ ⑧ ⑨ ⑩

3. I spend my day doing productive and meaningful work.

① ② ③ ④ ⑤ ⑥ ⑦ ⑧ ⑨ ⑩

4. I avoid complaining and focus on things I can control.

① ② ③ ④ ⑤ ⑥ ⑦ ⑧ ⑨ ⑩

5. I assume the best in my people and their intentions.

① ② ③ ④ ⑤ ⑥ ⑦ ⑧ ⑨ ⑩

6. I love what I do at work.

① ② ③ ④ ⑤ ⑥ ⑦ ⑧ ⑨ ⑩

7. I actively seek out diverse feedback from my team, peers, and leaders.

① ② ③ ④ ⑤ ⑥ ⑦ ⑧ ⑨ ⑩

8. I am constantly learning and developing my skills.

① ② ③ ④ ⑤ ⑥ ⑦ ⑧ ⑨ ⑩

9. I am consistently being coached and developed.

① ② ③ ④ ⑤ ⑥ ⑦ ⑧ ⑨ ⑩

10. I remove distractions and prevent fire drills from my people.

① ② ③ ④ ⑤ ⑥ ⑦ ⑧ ⑨ ⑩

What were the top areas that you scored low in?

What were your top strengths?

If you could pick only one or two areas to begin working on, where would you focus on addressing your personal vortex?

What question and response surprised you the most? Why?

You just took the first step to addressing the vortex. You acknowledged the parts that are affecting you and your team the most. Now, you can embrace fresh solutions to improve yourself and your culture. Your life can be better. It's a choice you can make. As you read on, you'll find practical tools and resources to help you shift yourself, your team, and your organization away from the pull of the destructive vortex.

CHAPTER 3

The New Rules of Coaching

If the only tool you have is a hammer, it is tempting to treat everything as if it were a nail.

—ABRAHAM MASLOW, *THE PSYCHOLOGY OF SCIENCE: A RECONNAISSANCE*

When I facilitate coaching workshops, I ask the group to define coaching. Inevitably, there are about as many definitions of coaching as there are people in the room. These definitions range greatly from simple feedback methods to sophisticated certified coaching programs. Let's explore a few definitions I hear most often. Then we'll discuss the new rules of coaching.

THE SOCRATIC COACH

The purist in the coaching industry will argue that coaching is Socratic in nature. Simply stated, the coach provides a series of meaningful questions that allows the coachee to become aware of their solution. There are few answers provided by this type of coach, just effective questions that promote reflection. In many cases, the coach doesn't have to be an expert in the field of the topics they are coaching. They see themselves as experts in the coaching process. Life coaches and executive coaches often fall more into this style of coaching. There is usually a certification process and credentials that come with those seeking to work in this form of coaching. Some people feel this type of coaching seems a lot like a counseling session with a psychologist. One of the key distinctions between a counselor and a coach is that a counselor will tend to focus on past events that drive present behavior. A coach, on the other hand, tends to ask, "Now what?" Yes, events and decisions have brought you to this point, but the coach wants to know what you are going to do about your situation right now. They help the coachee create an action plan to move forward, regardless of historical events.

THE EXPERT COACH

Expert business coaching has emerged with a greater focus on mentorship. These business gurus provide guidance and direction based on goals the leader has set. They are more actively involved in looking over financials and employee profiles. They help guide strategy with sound advice from their personal experience. Out of this wealth of experience, they can help others avoid certain pitfalls and help the coachee fast-track reaching their goals. In many cases, they also provide more direct accountability.

THE TEACHER COACH

The common definition of coaching combines feedback and training. These coaches provide a transfer of knowledge. If you are doing something wrong, they will call it out, and if you need help with a technical skill, they will teach you how to perform the task. For example, a teacher coach might say, "This is how you do this task. Now you do it. I will observe you and provide direction based on what I see."

THE CYA COACH

The evolution of coaching in the corporate world over the last thirty years has greatly changed. In some organizations, the word "coaching" is synonymous with write-ups, counseling statements, and corrective action. Let's call it the "accountability method." In CYA coaching, the message is clear: you have failed at your job and need a formal verbal or written process to stimulate change. If change fails to happen quickly or adequately enough, then the company can use the tool as justification to terminate your employment. This type of coaching is the tool of choice for HR practitioners and senior leaders who want to quickly remedy a problem and avoid lawsuits. In theory, this type of coaching is designed as redemptive or helpful to get a wandering employee back on track. However, in many organizations, by the time these practices are utilized, the leader and HR team have already concluded they are working the team member out of the company. These three-strikes-and-you're-out-type methods can give coaching a bad name. With this type of coaching prevalent in the corporate world today, it is no wonder many see coaching as something to be avoided.

A BLENDED APPROACH

After many years listening to groups of leaders argue that their view of coaching is the correct one, I have concluded that coaching doesn't have to be a choice of a single method. In fact, I have found that the most effective coaches are those who use aspects from each definition. They implement the tool that best fits the circumstance. As important as a hammer is in the toolbox of a carpenter, the other tools can be just as critical, depending on the job. The same is true for a coach. The more tools you have and master in your toolbox, the more precise you can be in addressing problems.

Coaching is a skill that leaders are expected to perform and it's often stated in their job description, but there is little training and understanding around the subject. To help us simplify the topic, I offer this working definition:

Coaching is the process of providing feedback, training, mentoring, and collaboration to help others achieve better results.

For memory purposes, let's use a mnemonic device. If you take the first letters of each of the main points, feedback, training, mentoring, and collaboration, FTMC, you can memorize this statement—Fit The Method to the Circumstance.

Feedback, training, mentoring, and collaboration allow you to fit the method to the circumstance and use the best tool for each coaching opportunity. These are the essential tools we will explore in this book.

WHY MULTIPLE APPROACHES WORK

An intriguing article titled "The Future of Cancer" that appeared in the June 15, 2017 issue of *Fortune* magazine exemplifies why different approaches—or zones—to coaching are necessary.

Over the past century, cancer research has totally evolved. It used to be that everyone received a similar treatment. As time went on, oncologists began to wonder, "Why is this treatment not working? The same treatment worked for Jim, so why doesn't it work on Susie?" They eventually discovered there was more to the whole system of fighting cancer than just the shock-and-awe approach of traditional chemotherapies. Instead of a one-size-fits-all solution, the future of cancer treatment is based on using multiple approaches.

When targeted treatments are used, the results are impressive. For instance, there was a 34 percent improvement in overall survival rates in stage III trials for patients with metastatic melanoma. In addition, stage III clinical trials demonstrated that up to 40 percent of patients with metastatic melanoma, including those who had not responded to a certain kind of drug commonly used, responded to the targeted treatment. People they had basically given up on were now living years instead of just days, and many people were going into remission who normally wouldn't have.

This is the power of using a multipronged approach. It works for cancer, and it also works for coaching. Many organizations use just one coaching style. Some organizations use only feedback or training, some professional coaches use only collaboration, and some places use only a mentorship model. Using just one approach is limiting. If leaders use a blended approach of all four of the methods, they can better address each individual situation. This targeted philosophy allows them to coach more effectively.

The cookie-cutter approach works great for making cookies, and that's about it. A tailored coaching style in which you intertwine and utilize the different zones will get you much farther and give you better results.

THE FOUR COACHING ZONES

The four, core coaching disciplines—feedback, training, mentoring, and collaboration—may be viewed as individual coaching zones. Although the four zones can overlap at times, examining them separately helps us understand each one in-depth so we can learn to master each discipline completely.

Coaching is organic in nature. Processes can overlap and flow into each other. Each situation you encounter will vary and need reexamination. Unlike building a home that has some exact science and guidelines, dealing with human beings gets a lot more subjective. What worked last time will not always work this time. That's why these are zones and not steps. The goal isn't to progress through each method of coaching until you reach the last zone, but rather to understand each zone so you can use the right method when it's appropriate and move between them as needed.

Following is a quick summary of each of the four coaching zones. We will explore them in greater detail in the next few chapters. Although you will see the word "problem" used at times in some of the language and examples, understand that coaching is not just a method to address problems. Coaching at its core is about helping others develop professionally and personally to improve performance. Coaching addresses behaviors or obstacles that hold a person back from maximizing their efforts.

ZONE 1: FEEDBACK

Feedback occurs when a leader essentially says, "You have a problem. Go fix it."

In this zone, the person receiving feedback, who we can refer to as the coachee, doesn't necessarily have an awareness of the problem or concern that needs to be addressed. The coach provides awareness through the coaching process.

Feedback is the process of creating awareness in others that they can't see in themselves.

These observations provide both positive and negative insights that are affecting performance. The goal of feedback is to bring about awareness to help the individual address the behaviors or obstacles preventing them from reaching their full capacity. We all face the reality that we have blind spots about ourselves, our motives, and our behaviors, and how they affect others. This outside perspective from the coach shines a light on our blind spots and opens the door to enable change. The most important part of the feedback process is not the awareness itself, but through the awareness, change takes place, and we experience enhanced performance.

Feedback is an effective coaching tool when people haven't fixed a problem because they aren't aware it exists.

ZONE 2: TRAINING

Training is "You have a problem. Here's how to fix it."

In this zone, a leader points out a problem and then strategically offers the coachee knowledge, tools, and resources to help them fix it.

Training is the transferring of knowledge, information, and skills so a person can perform an expected task.

Training is a great tool to use when someone doesn't have the knowledge required to fix a problem on their own. It's effective for filling in the gaps when they're missing concrete pieces of necessary knowledge.

ZONE 3: MENTORING

Mentoring marks a shift in awareness. Instead of the leader bringing the problem to the team member's attention, the team member approaches the leader with the issue: "I have a problem. Fix me."

Mentoring is the process where two individuals enter into a learning relationship together that has focused objectives, established boundaries, and a clear timeline.

Mentoring is different from training because, while someone who provides training doesn't have to be an expert in the field they train, a mentor does. In Zone 3, a mentor must come from a wealth of experience and extensive knowledge in the area they're coaching. They can guide others through problems because they've been there and done that.

ZONE 4: COLLABORATION

Collaboration is "I have a problem. Help me fix myself." This zone gets into the areas of executive performance and developmental coaching in which the coach asks questions and lets the coachee self-discover and figure out how to fix the problem themselves.

Collaboration is the process of recognizing the power within others and helping them create their own solutions by providing the right awareness, support, and environment to implement change.

This zone is ideal when the team member doesn't need someone else telling them what to do because they already have the answer inside. The coach's job is to create awareness for the coachee to explore the situation differently and then help them find a solution on their own. This zone promotes introspection and helps people see things they haven't been able to see in order to gain a better understanding of what they already know.

OPTIMIZED COACHING

When all four zones are working together, we call this optimized coaching. Learning each of the four zones is a critical step to becoming a successful coach. You must also understand when to use each zone, based on the people, circumstances, and situation. Some call this the art of being savvy. The great horseman and teacher Pat Parelli puts it this way, "Savvy is knowing when to be, where to be, why to be, and what to do when you get there."

Optimized coaching is like that. The coach understands when and where to use a specific zone. They also understand how to tweak the zone depending on the situation. Leaders and managers must learn how each coaching tool works and know when, where, and how to use each one. Once you have mastered each of the zones and can quickly identify which zone to use in any circumstance, you will have broken the coaching code.

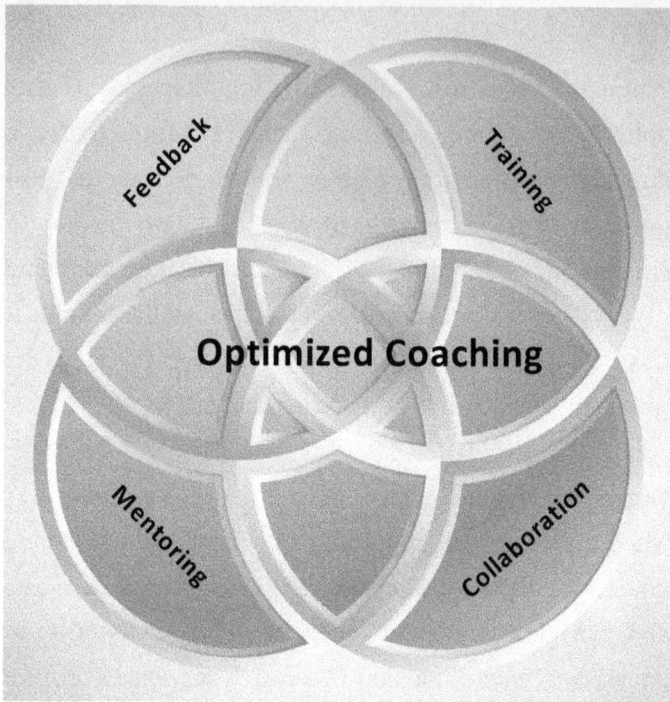

Optimized Coaching

(Feedback, Training, Mentoring, Collaboration)

THE IMPACT MODEL

Coaching zones vary in their potential impact and their risk to the individual being coached. The higher the zone, the greater potential for impact and the higher the risk to the individual. Therefore, Zones 1 and 2, feedback and training, inherently come with less risk and impact potential than do Zones 3 and 4, mentoring and collaboration.

For example, providing a team training on a new process that solves a problem has relatively minimal risk compared to collaborating with the team to engage them in developing their own process. Each approach may lead to a solution, but the risk to the individuals is much higher in the latter example.

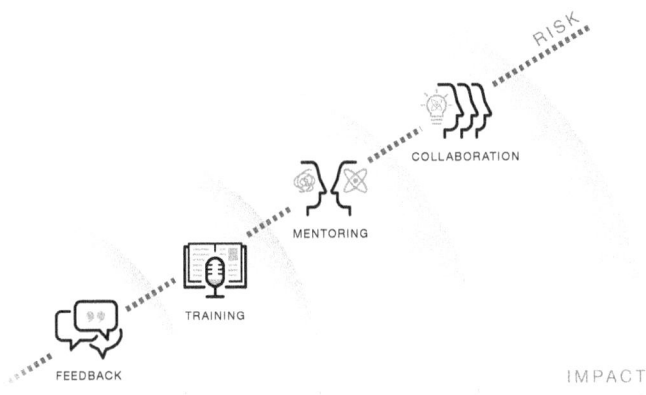

Leaders new to coaching may be tempted to jump straight to a higher zone of coaching to create impactful change quickly. In theory, this makes sense; however, foundational elements must first be in place to create a positive, rather than a negative, impact. Groundwork, including the development of trust, safety, and self-awareness is required to decrease the risk and increase the chances of successful, positive coaching in these higher zones.

Unfortunately, these additional requirements can intimidate new coaches. In my experience, an overwhelming majority of leaders tend to stay in Zones 1 and 2, feedback and training. They're easier, safer, and don't require a lot of change on the part of the coach or the organization but they focus, instead, on the behaviors of the coachee. This unwillingness to lay the groundwork and venture into higher coaching zones prevents leaders from fully developing their coaching skills and allowing their teams the full benefits of optimized coaching.

THE COACH IN THE MIRROR

Now that you understand the coaching zones, consider your own coaching methods. Most leaders, unaware of the four coaching zones, believe they spend a lot of time mentoring and collaborating with their people. However, if they analyzed their coaching experiences and compared them to the definitions of feedback, training, mentoring, and collaboration, they would discover they rely heavily on the low-risk, low-impact zones, rarely committing their efforts to higher zones that could deliver much greater results.

Having the same conversations with the same people is a telltale sign you're only coaching in the lower zones. Issues with low engagement and high turnover can also indicate a dependence on low-impact coaching zones.

Feedback and training have their place in your coaching code, but until you take steps to listen to the needs of your people, which occurs in mentoring and collaboration, and engaging them to create their own solutions, such as with developmental collaboration, your impact as a coach is limited.

To break the coaching code, start with an honest appraisal of your current coaching status. Then, commit to become the coach you were meant to be.

CHAPTER 4

Five Truths About Coaching

I believe people make their own luck by great preparation and good strategy.[1]

—JACK CANFIELD

Now that we have defined coaching and the different coaching zones, let's discuss five truths about coaching. Understanding and accepting these truths will facilitate and accelerate your own development as a coach and mastery of optimized coaching.

---

1   Douglas Vigliotti, "Only Losers Rely on Luck to Increase Sales," LinkedIn, January 9, 2017, accessed October 31, 2017, https://www.linkedin.com/pulse/only-losers-rely-luck-increase-sales-douglas-vigliotti.

TRUTH #1: COACHING IS EASY—BUT IT'S JUST AS EASY NOT TO DO IT

Many traditional coaching books talk about how difficult coaching is. Then coaching professionals wonder why leaders avoid adopting new strategies, like coaching, into their management styles. The reality is that every leader can be a great coach. From my perspective, anything we have the ability to do is easy. It is also easy not to do it.

Just like dieting, where it's easy to eat the right foods, it's also easy to eat the wrong foods. When faced with whether to eat a piece of cake or vegetables, we may feel the decision is difficult. But the difficult part of this is not the actual process of chewing food and digesting. It is the mental barriers where our bodies prefer the effects of sugary goodness over the healthier alternative. You can make good coaching choices, but you also can make bad ones. The question is, which choice will you make?

I used to tell leaders that being an effective coach and an ineffective coach takes the same effort, energy, time, and resources, but I was wrong. Being an effective, impactful coach takes less time and less energy once we master the skills. If breaking the coaching code is easier than what you're doing right now, why wouldn't you do it?

TRUTH #2: YOU'RE NOT BROKEN, AND NEITHER IS YOUR TEAM

Many times, when we feel ineffective, we blame our organization. We demonize our company and the people in it, and we assume if something isn't working, the whole thing is bad. However, that's not how organizations work. There might be aspects that don't work, but that doesn't mean everything is broken, and it doesn't mean you, your team, or your culture is broken. It simply means some things need to be addressed. Think of it as a web where everything is connected, but if one section is weak, the web can still do its job. Instead of having a tear-down-and-overhaul mindset, it is important to see the organization and your team as a web with some weakened portions that need strengthening.

Recall the story of Jen from the introduction: she went from shining star to being let go by her organization. Think about how Jen responded when she was struggling to meet the demands of her organization or how I responded when I wasn't happy with my new boss. At times, when we're not respected, appreciated, and liked, we think the answer is to scrap everything and go somewhere else instead of changing the things we can. We might think we're stuck in the worst culture ever, and perhaps there are aspects of the culture that are bad. But if we start treating things as if they're not broken but just need some tweaks, we may find powerful change is possible.

Seeing your team as broken, and taking dramatic steps to fix it, can have dire consequences. Early in my career, I took over a sales team that I thought was broken. My first response was to overhaul everything, so I told my team of managers to write down the names of all their people, and then mark which ones they wanted to keep and who they'd get rid of if they could. Using these lists as a guide, I replaced 75 percent of the salespeople. You would think my sales managers would be thrilled, yet 60 percent of those managers left within six months. I thought if I got rid of the bad people, I could easily replace them with good people. What I realized, years later, was that it was less about my people's inability to be appropriate team members and more about my inability to be the leader they needed.

I was asking the wrong questions, so I was getting the wrong answers. Instead of asking, "Who are the wrong people?" I should have been asking, "Who do I need to be in order to be the right leader for these people?" I was trying to force my people to be the right people for the type of leader I wanted to be instead of simply changing the kind of leader I was.

The perfect team doesn't magically exist out there, but you can take steps to create and build a highly effective team. People are willing—begging even—to change if you just work with them and see their incredible potential. People are unique individuals with their own special qualities, and leaders must be willing to work with them to bring out the best in who they are.

TRUTH #3: YOU'RE ALREADY COACHING EVERY DAY BUT MAY NOT BE GETTING THE DESIRED RESULTS

Coaching isn't something extra to add to your workload because you're already coaching in some form or fashion. You communicate to your team throughout the day in person, on the phone, in email, and in meetings. You also communicate with them nonverbally.

As a leader, people are watching you constantly. You may not be coaching them formally, but your communication—or lack of communication—speaks to them, and your silence can be louder than raising your voice to them.

Your team learns from the decisions you make every day. Becoming more self-aware and intentional in your words, behaviors, and actions affects how your team sees you, because you are the role model against which they gauge the appropriateness of their own words, behaviors, and actions. People are incredibly observant of their leaders, so be sure to set an example you would like them to follow. As a leader, you should set the bar high.

TRUTH #4: EVERYONE NEEDS A COACH

In Chapter 1, "The Greatest Competitive Advantage," we talked about how the best of the best have coaches. In every sport or industry, top performers have someone outside of themselves providing direction and guidance to help them improve performance.

What about the people who just want to be average? We hear people say all the time they just want to show up, do their job, and go home. They aren't looking to grow, nor do they want to change the world. They do enough to get by, and if they can run in the middle of the pack, they think that is good enough.

This mindset works until it doesn't. At certain points, we all face moments when we hit walls and we need support to continue. No matter how hard people may try, no one is exempt from wanting to grow and evolve. The world is constantly changing and requires us to change with it if we hope to survive. Many people who claim they don't want to be coached also go through life as victims. They feel powerless over their decisions and beholden to someone else to make choices for them. Then, they blame circumstances and other people for why they are not happy in their lives. I may refuse to exercise and take care of my health. This doesn't change the reality that one day those choices will affect my body. There are those who will refuse to be coached. This decision will eventually affect their development, performance, and career.

TRUTH #5: IT'S NOT ABOUT GENIUS—IT'S ABOUT PRACTICE

Coaching doesn't take a genius. Many of us think people are natural-born leaders or natural coaches, but they're not. They've just learned and practiced the right skills. They may have had more opportunities along the way and be more gifted in certain areas that helped them succeed, but overall, the idea of geniuses making miracles happen is, in my opinion, a farce. The key to many of the geniuses who have made a difference in our world is the number of hours they've put into something, not their natural talent. This goes back to psychologist K. Anders Ericsson's 10,000-hour rule.[2] What Ericsson and his team of researchers found was that many people considered "natural" geniuses and athletes had something in common: 10,000 hours of practice. Their research showed the status of industry leaders and experts in many fields had less to do with natural talent and genius, and more to do with opportunities to practice. They claim that even people like the musician Mozart didn't hit his peak until after 10,000 hours of practice.

The good news is you don't need to spend 10,000 hours on coaching to be an expert. By just taking small steps, you can make significant change happen. Most managers do not have the time or the inclination to become a master coach. However, they do have the time to be an impactful leader that can foster exceptional performance.

---

2   Malcolm Gladwell, *Outliers* (New York: Back Bay, 2008), 38 and 42.

FIVE TRUTHS OF COACHING

Understanding and accepting these coaching truths will facilitate your development as a coach.

Coaching Truth #1: Coaching is easy, but it's just as easy not to do it.

Coaching Truth #2: You're not broken and neither is your team.

Coaching Truth #3: You're already coaching every day but may not be getting the desired results.

Coaching Truth #4: Everyone needs a coach.

Coaching Truth #5: It's not about genius—it's about practice.

PART I CONCLUSION

Many people think coaching requires giant leaps of progress, but tweaking one or two small things can make a significant difference. Statistically, people who make their bed every day are more productive. Does that mean if you don't make your bed, you won't achieve high results? Of course not. It's about the mindset. Small actions can trigger giant leaps in our results. It's not doing big things but doing small things consistently that will help you get where you want to be.

Accepting these five truths allows you to embrace what is possible through coaching. You can do this.

PART I QUESTIONS FOR REFLECTION

1. Think of a problem you're currently struggling with at work. How might you engage the people closest to the problem to come up with their own solution?

2. How can you enlist the five elements of maximizing top talent to foster a culture of high engagement and retention?

3. Does your company utilize coaching as a corrective action? How can you change the dialogue and help leaders see coaching in a positive light?

4. Do you contribute to your company's vortex? What can you do today to make your employees' jobs less cumbersome and allow them to be more productive?

5. Where are you struggling in the vortex? Who can you reach out to for help with those problems? While you're developing your coaching skills, look for people who can coach you as well.

6. Thinking back on your most recent coaching experiences, which coaching zones did you use? Describe each situation and the zone you used.

7. Do you believe you used the right coaching zone for each situation? Why or why not?

8. If you were to have those same coaching opportunities again, which zones would you use this time? Why? How do you think your choice of zone might affect your results?

9. What steps can you take right now to become a different type of coach?

10. Who do you need to become for your people to perform at their best?
11. How much brilliance are you willing to allow your people to experience by changing the way you approach them and their development?

Part II

FEEDBACK

CHAPTER 5

Introduction to Zone 1: Feedback

Feedback often tells you more about the person who is giving it than about you.

—STEPHEN R. COVEY

Zone 1, feedback, occurs when a leader essentially says, "You have a problem. Go fix it."

In this zone, the person receiving feedback, who we can refer to as the coachee, doesn't necessarily have an awareness of the problem or concern that needs to be addressed. The coach provides awareness through the coaching process.

Feedback is the process of creating awareness in others that they can't see in themselves.

These observations provide both positive and negative insights that are affecting performance. The goal of feedback is to bring about awareness to help the individual address the behaviors or obstacles preventing them from reaching their full capacity. We all face the reality that we have blind spots about ourselves, our motives, and our behaviors, and how they affect others. This outside perspective from the coach shines a light on our blind spots and opens the door to enable change. The most important part of the feedback process is not the awareness itself, but through the awareness, change takes place and we experience enhanced performance.

Feedback is an effective coaching tool when people haven't fixed a problem because they aren't aware it exists.

Feedback is often not used effectively, either in the giving or receiving. There may be a lot of talking and information exchanged but little or no effective feedback. Effective feedback creates change and drives new results. Feedback, if done correctly, empowers those who receive it. Basically, a lot of leaders talk *at* people as opposed to giving effective feedback.

People often avoid giving feedback, but the cost of silence is high. As stated in Tom Rath's *StrengthsFinder*, a Gallup poll found that if a manager primarily ignores an employee, the chance of that person being actively disengaged is 40 percent.[1] So if your manager decides they don't want to

---

1   Tom Rath, *StrengthsFinder 2.0* (New York: Gallup, 2007).

rock the boat and cause problems, and doesn't provide you with feedback, there's a 40 percent chance you'll become actively disengaged. "Actively disengaged" doesn't mean you're checked out, hiding in your cubicle, but that you are actively working against the system to sabotage the organization. The same poll found that if your manager focuses only on your weaknesses, there's a 22 percent chance of you being actively disengaged, meaning that silence is more damaging than negative feedback.

Leaders need to provide a balanced approach to feedback that engages employees with both positive reinforcement and opportunities for growth.

FEEDBACK AS A WEAPON: LATOYA'S LAND MINES

Latoya was a VP who thought everyone wanted her input and opinion on everything. She thought her feedback empowered people, but she used her unfiltered comments as a tool against them. When I think about Latoya, I recall her sharp, quick steps coming down the hall as she did her morning walk-around, popping in to say *hey* to each team member. It was almost as if her feet were attacking the floor, and that's how she used feedback too: to attack people. She did what I call "swoop and poop," where she would stop, drop her feedback, and be gone. People began to fear these feedback drops.

When you get feedback like this, it's about power and not

about what's in your best interest. People like Latoya don't use positive feedback very often, which is another reason her team dreaded her feedback swoops. Her comments were usually negative in tone, and a compliment from her was like a small miracle.

While Latoya loved giving feedback, she didn't like receiving it. On one occasion, I was asked to provide some coaching feedback to her. Partway through, I had to stop the conversation and say, "Giving you feedback is wounding to me."

"What do you mean?" she asked.

"You make me feel like it's an argument or like I have to prove my comments. If you really want feedback from people, you need to learn to receive it."

THE RULES OF FEEDBACK

A balanced approach to feedback follows these five essential rules.

RULE #1: PEOPLE VALUE FEEDBACK ABOVE ALL ELSE

American Express did a survey to find out what workers wanted most from employers. Forty-six percent of those surveyed said they wanted personal feedback, compared to 32 percent who said they wanted financial rewards. As the article states, "Promotions and pay raises are no longer granted to workers solely based on years of service. Performance has become the catalyst for getting ahead in most companies. As employees see this, they naturally want to know how they are doing."[2]

People want feedback because they know it will help them achieve more. It will help them grow, get where they want to go, and get more out of their work relationships. Oftentimes, leaders think they just need to give employees a Starbucks gift card or a trophy. Recognition is important in the work environment, but feedback is what people really want, whether it's positive or critical.

RULE #2: FEEDBACK HAS LESS TO DO WITH CONTENT AND MORE TO DO WITH INTENT

There is a drastic difference between intent and content when it comes to feedback. At times, a leader may spend a great deal of effort deciding how to spin the content they need to share. Even if the words are articulated well, the message may not be received well. On the other hand, someone close to us may share an observation that is blunt and insensitive; however, the person hearing it will receive it openly. Why? The difference is in how we interpret the intention of the one communicating the message. If we believe

---

2   Patti Hathaway, *Feedback Skills for Leaders* (Boston: Thomson Learning, 2006).

the messenger has our best interest in mind, they can share just about anything with us. If we doubt their intention, it doesn't matter how well something is said. We will often become defensive or reluctant to hear it. As many have said before: people don't care what you know until they know that you care.

When people think about giving feedback, they worry about how their words will be received, and they agonize over how to phrase it the best way. But people receiving feedback don't care about that; they care about the intentions behind your words. You may have great feedback, but unless people think your intent is good, they don't care about the content.

Think about how you feel when your spouse gives you feedback on something. You know they have your best interests at heart, and you trust their intentions. You trust their words and accept them, whereas if the same feedback came from someone you didn't trust, you probably wouldn't be open to receiving it. Of course, if you and your spouse are experiencing problems in your relationship, you may not trust their feedback, but generally speaking, you are more likely to accept feedback from a person you trust.

RULE #3: WE TEND TO EXPECT EVERYONE TO SEE FEEDBACK THE WAY WE DO

This rule is especially important today because we're about

to have five generations in the workforce at the same time, which has never happened. These are the traditionalists, the baby boomers, the Generation Xers, the millennials (also known as Generation Y), and Generation Z, which is preparing to enter the workforce. Each group sees feedback from their perspective, and they often blame other generational groups for why the work environment isn't the way it needs to be.

My neighbor, a boomer about four years out from retirement, was talking to me about some millennials he supervises. He said, "I just don't get them. They need constant reassurance. They're whiny, needy, and don't take initiative." Then he said, "Now, I've got some other people in their fifties who work for me, and they are so easy to work with. They get the culture. They understand. They're not needy, and they are the most effective." Essentially what he was really saying was that anyone who wasn't like him was difficult to work with and difficult to give feedback to. This is a common trap people fall into because we tend to see the world one way and expect everyone else to see it that way too.

In his TEDx Talk,[3] Paul Rulkens tells a story about Albert Einstein. In 1942, Einstein was teaching a class at Oxford. He was walking with his teaching assistant, and the assistant

---

3   Paul Rulkens, "Why the Majority is Always Wrong," *TEDxMaastricht*, October 21, 2014, video, 11:25, accessed October 24, 2017, https://www.youtube.com/watch?v=VNGFep6rncY.

asked, "Professor Einstein, did you just give your senior physics students the same test you gave them last year?"

Einstein said, "Yes, it was the same test."

"Why would you do that?" the assistant asked.

"Because the answers have changed," Einstein said.

The questions were the same, but the answers had changed. It's the same concept that Marshall Goldsmith addresses in his book, *What Got You Here Won't Get You There*. You may believe the rules are the rules and they never change, but that's not true.[4] While the questions are the same, the answers change. The way we look at feedback has to change too, and there isn't just one way of looking at it. Different generations, people, and entire companies view feedback differently.

"Tell Me What I'm Doing Wrong" Feedback

Older generations tend to have a "Tell me what I'm doing wrong" mindset. They're more interested in the negative than the positive, and they expect a more structured approach to feedback, like formal reviews as opposed to informal feedback chats.

---

4   Marshall Goldsmith and Mark Reiter, What Got You Here Won't Get You There: How Successful People Become Even More Successful (New York: Hyperion, 2007).

"Tell Me What I Need to Hear" Feedback

Others prefer immediate, specific feedback. They want it raw, candid, and right away. This approach to feedback is common among Gen Xers. They want you to tell them what they're doing wrong and then get out of their way, so they can fix it. Their mindset is "I'm listening to you. Just tell me what I need to hear, and I'll make it happen." This is where feedback starts to become a more informal process.

Fair Feedback

The final group is composed mainly of younger folks coming into the workplace, and they care about fairness. Feedback for them is consistent, informal, and provided in a collaborative style. They want to share in the feedback discussion as well, and they view feedback as a positive thing.

While coaching some people in their twenties for an organization, I asked them what they would change about the organization.

One young man said, "Well, my boss yells at me all the time."

Others in the group nodded in agreement.

"Yelling? Really?" I said. "Tell me about that."

"Yeah, he raises his voice and tells me what I'm doing wrong," he said.

"He actually yells at you?" I questioned.

"Well, he just tells me how bad I'm doing."

What these people viewed as yelling, others would call giving negative feedback. It was a totally different perspective. These younger generations want consistent feedback and want to hear the positives, but negative feedback can come across as yelling to them. Now you could complain about these young people's tender egos, but that isn't productive. The goal in effective feedback is to move people, relationships, and results. A balanced approach to feedback takes different views of feedback into consideration. You shouldn't fight against people's views but, instead, try to match your feedback style with whatever the person you're coaching needs.

Effective leaders do things differently in different situations. They understand that to communicate in an optimized way, they must shift and change their style to meet each person's needs. They tailor their feedback so the person receiving it perceives it in the best way.

RULE #4: PEOPLE CANNOT ARGUE WITH PERSONAL FEELINGS AND THOUGHTS

Leaders sometimes wonder why their people get defensive and are not responsive and open to feedback, and in many cases, it comes down to the language used. For instance, saying, "You did this," sounds like an accusation, but saying, "I feel this" or "I think this," sounds like personal feelings and thoughts. People can't argue with "I" statements because they represent a perspective, and everyone has their own perspective. However, when a leader uses "you" statements, such as "You did this," or "You are this," people respond negatively and become defensive. If your feedback isn't tied to facts, it's hard to receive. Avoid assumptions and generalizations.

Leaders should have a 10 percent doubt factor when giving feedback—that is, 10 percent of them needs to think, "I might be wrong about this." Having that little bit of doubt allows for the understanding that the feedback should be a conversation as opposed to absolute dogma. Saying things like, "I feel I'm on the right track here, but I could be wrong," introduces a little bit of humility that enables others to receive and be open to the feedback dialogue so they can choose what to do with the information.

RULE #5: EFFECTIVE FEEDBACK LEADS TO ACTIONABLE STEPS AND/OR IDEAS FOR CHANGE

Effective feedback is designed to help individuals change behaviors and improve performance. Feedback provides ways to see the situation from a different perspective. By seeing things differently, it fosters a new way to approach problems. Through this awareness, individuals can establish actionable steps to create positive change.

FIVE RULES OF FEEDBACK

A balanced approach to feedback follows five essential rules.

Feedback Rule #1: People value feedback above all else.

Feedback Rule #2: Feedback has less to do with content and more to do with intent.

Feedback Rule #3: We tend to expect everyone to see feedback the way we do, but that's simply not the case.

Feedback Rule #4: People cannot argue with personal feelings and thoughts.

Feedback Rule #5: Effective feedback leads to actionable steps and/or ideas for change.

CHAPTER 6

The SEEE
Feedback Model

Failure is merely feedback that there is something blocking the
path of the emergence and expansion of the greatest version
of yourself.

—MOTHER THERESA

To give effective feedback, I recommend the four-step SEEE
feedback model, which stands for Specify, Express, Explore,
and Explain.

THE **SEEE** FEEDBACK MODEL

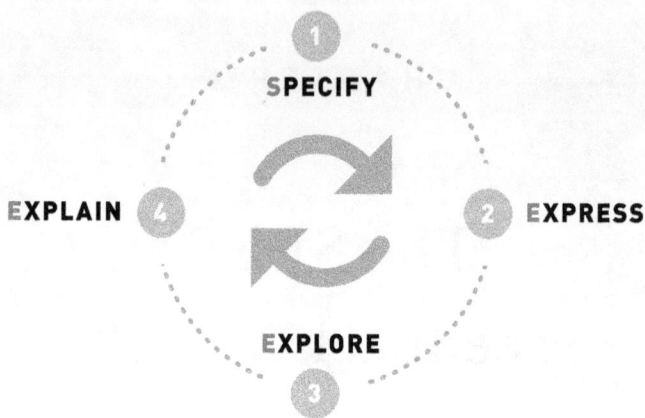

1. **SPECIFY**
2. **EXPRESS**
3. **EXPLORE**
4. **EXPLAIN**

SPECIFY

In the specify step, describe the situation—what has happened to warrant the feedback. Focus on the facts and tailor the conversation to the specific person and events to maximize your feedback's impact.

Begin with the facts to avoid putting the team member on the defensive. The facts are black and white. If a manager starts by using subjective assumptions or impressions, the approach can instantly spark an argument. An example of the specify step would be to say, "Here's what I heard you say," followed by what you heard. Or you might say, "When I watched your recent meeting this week, I noticed this," and then describe the situation. The specify stage is important for establishing the big picture of what you saw and heard. This is the facts only, not the story.

EXPRESS

Then you move to express. In this step, you express how you felt about or interpreted the situation—your take on the events. This is where you would say, "Based on what I saw, I feel you did this," or "The way I interpreted it was this." This is where you state your view and opinion of the situation or event based on the information available to you at the time.

EXPLORE

In the third step, explore, you offer alternatives or suggestions:

- "Here's what I recommend."
- "I suggest you try this."
- "Next time, I would like you to do this."

The explore step is also an opportunity to ask clarifying questions if needed. You shouldn't try to dominate the conversation, but clarify your interpretation of the facts by asking questions like,

- "Can you help me understand the reason you said this?"
- "Could you walk me through the process you chose?"
- "I noticed you didn't follow up with that customer. Can you help me understand what happened?"

The main objective of the explore phase is focusing on solutions, not criticism. For example, you would not say, "Hey, your comments really irritated me!" This is an attack more than a discussion about alternative behavior. Although their behavior may have irritated you, the focus should remain on the new behavior you want to see. Compare that statement with, "Here are some things you could do differently next time that could help change the way the customer responds to you." When you focus on solutions instead of criticism, it shows you have good intentions and have your team member's best interests in mind instead of your own.

EXPLAIN

The fourth step in the SEEE Model is explain. In this stage, you tie the feedback back to the goals and shared purpose. Because the purpose of feedback is to increase results, you need to draw those connections between your feedback and desired outcome. Essentially, you want to make sure the person receiving the feedback understands how their actions can impact the organization's results.

In the explain stage, express your sincerity and support. This is an opportunity to show you want to partner with your team member and help them. To show this support, say things like, "I know we're both committed to hitting this goal. I want to partner with you as you are growing in this role," and "What else can I do to help you?"

Finally, if there's going to be a follow-up, establish that at the explain phase. "Hey, I would like us to follow up tomorrow to make sure you're feeling good with your new process."

Feedback that utilizes all four of these SEEE steps would look like this. "I noticed you have been coming in late the last few days. Sometimes, I feel you don't see your job as a priority. I recognize that you have some issues happening in your personal life, but you being here on time helps us achieve our goals and take care of our customers. We both are committed to achieving our metrics and offering an exceptional customer experience. When you're not here on time, our customers have to wait longer. It drops our customer satisfaction scores. And ultimately, they are less likely to purchase additional services and products. This affects your paycheck and mine. Can I get your commitment to be on time going forward?"

Let's take a moment to practice the SEEE Model. Think about a coaching session that has either happened recently or needs to take place. Using the SEEE Model, fill in the following blanks:

Specify: What are the facts in the situation? What happened?

....

....

....

Express: Based on the facts, how did you interpret the team member's actions? How did it make you feel? This is your chance to tell your story.

....

....

....

Explore: What additional questions need to be answered concerning the situation? What options would you suggest to address the team member's behavior?

....

....

....

Explain: How does this change in behavior tie back to shared goals between the team member and yourself? What can you do to partner with the team member in the process? What follow-up is necessary now and/or in the future?

....

....

....

There are many effective feedback models available. I believe SEEE provides the critical elements to help create a safe and productive environment for feedback to take place. The most important part of any feedback model is to use it consistently. When a manager attempts to wing it, feedback can quickly become more critical and less productive. Comments turn from fact-based observations to feelings and assumptions. And instead of offering targeted solutions, the manager may provide generalities that can cause more harm than good.

CHAPTER 7

Feedback Mistakes to Avoid

What we see depends mainly on what we look for.

—SIR JOHN LUBBOCK

Following the five rules of feedback and utilizing the SEEE Model will put you on a path to effective feedback that can unlock the potential within your team while creating a healthier company culture. However, leaders often make feedback mistakes that can detract from their employees' success. Let's talk about some of these mistakes and how to avoid them.

VAGUE FEEDBACK

When feedback is vague, it's hard to make it actionable. For example, if you say, "I feel you are really not putting enough time into your work. You need to work harder," your coachee might wonder, "Putting enough time into what, exactly? What do you mean by working harder? Working longer hours? Doing better quality work?" Vague statements do not help the person know what specifically needs to be addressed. In fact, this kind of feedback can isolate the person and lead to assumptions and frustration, since the coachee hasn't been provided with clear feedback or instructions on how to make appropriate changes. Think about how often team members have received some vague feedback from their leader. They assumed they knew what it meant and ran off to fix the problem. Later, they realized their actions not only failed to fix the issue but perhaps made the situation worse.

Valuable feedback is specific and actionable. If you're going to bring something up, do it in a way that allows people to address it.

This applies to positive feedback as well. If you tell your team members, "Great job! Keep up the excellent work," without specifying what that excellent work is, they'll have no idea what they did or what they're supposed to continue doing. Compare that to a more specific example, like, "Great job on following up with the client concerning their bill and communicating with the VPs about our next steps in the process. I received a lot of positive feedback from the team. They appreciated that." Being more specific adds power to the feedback.

FEEDBACK FROM THE WRONG PERSON

Before giving feedback, ask yourself, "Am I the right person to be having this conversation?"

For example, if Amelia has a problem with another member of the team, she might approach her manager and say, "Did you hear this about Francisco? You need to deal with this. Here's what he needs to know."

Instead of giving Francisco feedback, it might be more appropriate and effective for the manager to say to Amelia, "Well, that's some great feedback. Since you are the one who heard Francisco say this and are directly affected by his behaviors, I think it would be best coming from you." In that way, the manager turns it back on Amelia to have a healthy dialogue with Francisco.

Now the manager can turn the opportunity to coaching Amelia on how to provide feedback to a peer. Coaching often involves these kinds of situations, and as the leader, you might have to coach Amelia on how to address issues and have healthy feedback conversations. Depending on the situation, you might also ask, "Would you like to have that conversation on your own, or would you like me to be a part of it with you?"

One way or another, Amelia and Francisco are going to have the conversation. Even if you are present, the feedback will still come primarily from Amelia. This approach to feedback stops gossip and issues within your team and helps keep your team members' relationships healthy by having the people who are truly involved in the situation—Francisco and Amelia—sit down together. The benefits to this are incredible. First, this empowers Amelia to deal with her own problems. It builds confidence in her ability instead of her dependence on you, her manager, to solve her problems. Second, it keeps the relationship between Amelia and Francisco healthy. If you gave Francisco that feedback instead, he would feel as if he'd been snitched on, and that would affect the trust within your team. On the other hand, when Amelia and Francisco talk about the issue together, Francisco will feel valued and that his relationship with Amelia is healthy enough to endure feedback dialogues.

Open dialogues among team members create an environment of trust and safety. They create an environment where people can make mistakes and have healthy conflict instead of letting issues fester and cause additional problems.

ATTACKING PEOPLE INSTEAD OF PROBLEMS

In many cases, coaching goes wrong because the coach attacks the person instead of the behavior or the situation. No matter what zone you're in, you must attack the problem, not the person.

You must make it clear it's the policy, procedure, behavior, or idea you're attacking, not the person. If the person you're coaching feels attacked, they will shut down. That person will no longer be open to the dialogue, and the conversation will grind to a halt. In these scenarios, people dig in, refusing to change, and there's no possibility for a positive outcome when two people get emotionally hooked like that. Feedback should be about behaviors and tangible things, not about attacking people.

TOO MUCH NEGATIVE FEEDBACK AND NOT ENOUGH POSITIVE

It's so easy to see the negative. We're often blind to the positive. As a leader, it's important to express gratitude, appreciation, and support along with guidance toward improvement. Our bodies are designed with a negative slant. It kept people alive in prehistoric times. People were on constant alert, waiting for danger to present itself behind the next tree or bush. However, today, we may not have the same dangers walking down the street, but the negative slant remains. For example, you will notice the news will run far more negative stories than positive. Magazines capture readers by providing stories of human frailty and failure more than success and goodwill. In fact, one study found that when a marriage focused too much on negative comments, it was far more likely to end in divorce. But in the best marriages, couples tend to focus on providing positive comments to their spouse or partner with the occasional negative comment. The study found the best split was five to one—five positive comments to one negative one.[1]

The same rule applies between managers and team members. If the manager focuses too much on negative feedback, sometimes masked as constructive criticism, the team member is much more likely to become disengaged or even leave the organization.

Think about your last performance review. Do you remember the positive comments or the one or two items you were called out to correct? We tend to forget the positive moments and revisit our failures over and over in our minds. This does not mean we are to focus only on strengths. It does mean we should appropriately balance our feedback with more time given to the positive.

You still need to coach the negative but balance it with the positive. To truly balance your feedback, you can't do fifty-fifty of positive and negative. Remember, it takes five positive comments to offset one negative comment. How can you bring more positives back into your work environment to start shifting behaviors and results?

---

1   Hara Estroff Marano, "Our Brain's Negative Bias: Why Our Brains Are More Highly Attuned to Negative News," *Psychology Today*, June 20, 2003, accessed February 25, 2018, https://www.psychologytoday.com/articles/200306/our-brains-negative-bias.

While you need to give both positive and negative feedback, you should not combine the two types, or the negative feedback may be lost. Mixing critical concerns with positive feedback is confusing to the person you're speaking to. They aren't sure whether they're supposed to take steps to remedy a situation, or if you're telling them that all is well. With no clear direction, the person receiving the feedback isn't likely to take steps to change anything.

For example, a leader might say to a team member, "You are a great employee. In fact, you're one of the best on the team. Here's one thing I would like you to work on with your customer satisfaction scores. Other than that, you're just great!" The leader may think they've made the issue clear, but the team member walks away feeling like they're doing a great job and there is no issue to be addressed. Then, when there's no improvement, the manager doesn't understand why the team member didn't follow up. It often escapes our minds to think that part of the reason the team member fails to improve is not their unwillingness to change but a lack of clarity in our ability to provide effective feedback.

INSINCERE FEEDBACK: MARIO'S MISTAKE

Mario was a marketing director whose team had the lowest employee-satisfaction scores in the company. When I asked him what he thought was going on, Mario said, "My people keep saying they need more positive reinforcement and feedback."

I asked him what he was doing about the issue, and he said, "Well, I keep a little tab right here. Every time someone comes into my office, I give them a positive statement, and then I check it off my calendar right here."

"How is that working for you?" I asked.

"Well, can you believe they're still complaining they don't get positive reinforcement?"

Yes, in fact, I could believe that. This seemed like a clear case where the content of the feedback wasn't having any effect because the right intent wasn't there. I asked Mario, "Do you really believe that it's good to give positive feedback?"

"Well, I never got positive feedback, so I don't think it's necessary."

"Do you think that mindset comes through when you're giving feedback?"

He admitted that it might be, and we discussed the importance of sincerity in his feedback. If he didn't believe in the importance of what he was saying and didn't believe it was going to help his people, then nothing he said would matter.

Mario's people would disregard it as false praise—something he was doing to check off a box, not because he meant it.

When you provide positive feedback, make sure it's sincere.

STRUCTURED FEEDBACK

Many official forms of coaching—like personal improvement plans (PIPs), counseling statements, write-ups, and other documentation tools—tend to fall under the feedback model because they follow a structured format and limit the flow of the conversation. These forms of feedback typically have actionable items, which fits the context of what feedback is supposed to provide. But in many cases of formalized feedback, people will experience negative repercussions if they don't follow through on the actionable items.

You need to approach feedback with your end goal in mind. In many cases, by the time coaches get to the point of using these formalized tools, they've already given up. They've decided this person isn't going to make it, and they're just checking off the legal requirements needed to fire that person. Feedback will not be effective in those situations.

You must believe there's a chance the person can make better decisions and improve for feedback to work. I've seen people get written up on performance improvement plans and then go on to become productive members of the organization again. The difference between success and failure came down to the coach's intention—what they believe about the person they coach and what they tried to achieve with those documents. When you're using formalized tools, how you approach coaching determines whether the person you coach will stay with the company or be terminated.

The success of these formalized documents is determined by what the coach has predetermined will happen. If the coach feels the team member can change, then often, it happens. If they feel there is no hope to save the employee, then that is usually the case. The coach will create a self-fulfilling prophecy based on their thoughts and beliefs.

These formalized tools scare people, and they're designed to. They're intended to make people realize they're in the danger zone, not living up to expectations, not hitting the numbers needed, not displaying the right behaviors, and so on.

In healthy coaching environments where there is regular one-on-one coaching feedback, feedback forms like PIPs often aren't necessary.

INCONSISTENT FEEDBACK

Even if an organization didn't use any of the other coaching zones and just gave consistent feedback, engagement scores and turnover would improve. People crave feedback, and providing people with feedback on their performance results in better performance and more engaged employees.

When you don't have consistent coaching, you tend to see consistent PIPs, counseling statements, and write-ups.

Too many organizations rely on a hope strategy. They hire people and then hope those people work out. The people get a certain period to make things work, and if they don't, the organization starts looking at how to work them out of the company and replace them with someone new. It's work up or work out, coach up or coach out.

Coaching shouldn't only happen when there's a problem. Coaching should be something positive, something to enhance and drive better performance, but instead, it has been used to beat people down. Think of coaching as nuclear power. Depending on how it's used, nuclear power can be highly efficient, clean energy that lights up the world, or it can destroy entire continents. Feedback is a powerful tool, but if it's misused, it has huge negative results. Used correctly, it has powerful implications that can drive impressive results and transform an organization. Companies need to make a paradigm shift in the way they view coaching to reap these benefits. Feedback is not just an HR tool. Feedback is a leadership tool that helps people get better results.

FEEDBACK TOO LATE: PETER'S PREDICAMENT

Peter, a sales manager, had twenty-four direct reports. He didn't think he had time to coach everyone on his team. I asked Peter how and with whom he spent his coaching time, and he said most of his energy went to his bottom performers. Then he focused on his top performers, and finally, he spent whatever time and energy he had left—which typically wasn't very much—on his middle performers.

"Have you noticed," I asked him, "that because you don't spend time on your middle performers, they eventually become your bottom performers?"

Eventually, Peter would spend time on his middle performers, but not until they became his low performers. If you don't engage your team in a coaching process of some kind, no matter how good they are, your top performers often become middle performers, and your middle performers become bottom performers. You don't usually hire bad people. They get that way over time. As a leader, you can prevent that from happening if you start coaching early on.

Shift your focus from trying to prevent bad results to trying to achieve better results. It's easier to bring people from the middle up than it is to save people at the bottom. If you have consistent, tailored coaching moments with your team, you won't have to spend as much time and energy on all the negative stuff that goes along with management and doesn't lead to better results.

PART II CONCLUSION

The difference between transformative feedback and ineffective feedback often comes down to one or two small mistakes that hurt the entire process. In many cases, these are not intentional, but things that have great effect on the entire process and experience.

For example, during some training in Colorado Springs, I was talking to a woman from the UK about the worst customer service experience she'd had. She was new to the United States and had heard wonderful things about the restaurant Sonic. For those not familiar with this fifties-style diner, it is based on the carhop concept. Customers drive up into these car stalls and order from their cars, and the server brings the food out to your vehicle. She and her husband went there to eat. One of the Sonic workers came out and went to all the other cars but completely ignored this woman and her husband. The two of them sat there for a while waiting to be helped but finally decided they weren't going to take this lack of customer service and left.

When she was done telling me her story, I asked, "Did you push the red button?" At Sonic, to place your order, you have to push the red button on the menu to call the kitchen.

Sure enough, it turned out she hadn't. What she'd thought of as the rudest customer service experience of her life had been a misunderstanding because she hadn't realized she needed to press the button. She later went back to Sonic, pushed the button, and enjoyed the experience.

It is not big mistakes that destroy a team or even a career. It is usually missing some small critical steps we need to take to make the entire process work effectively. Think about Latoya from Chapter 5. She thought her harsh and critical feedback was what people wanted and needed. Latoya's miscommunication with her team affected her results. She didn't take the time to figure out what her team was thinking or what they needed from her. If she had asked herself, "What's my intent here? What am I trying to accomplish with my people?" imagine what a difference it would have made in her feedback. She would have figured out she was focusing on criticism, not solutions. If she'd taken a step back, she also would have seen the negative way in which her feedback was perceived and how it was being used as an abuse of power. Instead of a weekly whipping of negative feedback, she could have had productive conversations and helped her people see things in ways they hadn't before. That's not what happened, though.

I worked with Latoya for about a year and a half, and in that time, almost everyone who worked for her when I started left the organization. Later, when I had a chance to talk to some of these people, they confessed they couldn't take Latoya anymore. Some said, "I would never work with Latoya again because she'll never learn to change." Until she's willing to work on herself and make some substantial changes, Latoya's behaviors are unlikely to shift. She didn't think anything was wrong with the way she was giving feedback and coaching her people. She thought she was a trusting person who was bringing much to the table. She lost the company great, talented people because she kept missing the "red button." The company thought Latoya was working with the wrong people, so they kept moving her around. But after a while, they realized she was the problem. Latoya wasn't willing to change, and she eventually lost her job.

One of the leaders I worked for used to say, "Either you take care of your people, or your people will take care of you." Latoya was focused on taking care of herself rather than her people, and her people took care of her. If you don't want to end up like Latoya, you must keep working on yourself, because eventually, you run out of places to hide, which will happen faster than you think. These days, you can't even hide by leaving a company because of the internet, social media, and sites like Glassdoor.com. Take care of your people and coach them appropriately before they take care of you.

WHAT IS FEEDBACK?

1. Feedback is the process of creating awareness in others that they can't see in themselves.

2. Feedback is initiated when a leader/coach essentially says, "You have a problem. Fix it."

3. In Zone 1, feedback, the team member/coachee isn't necessarily aware of the problem that needs to be addressed.

4. Feedback is an effective coaching tool when a team member hasn't fixed a problem because they either (a) aren't aware of it, (b) they are aware of the problem but are not aware of the seriousness of the situation, perhaps because they do not understand the expectations of their leadership, or (c) they are aware of the problem but don't know what to do about it.

5. The leader/coach provides awareness through the feedback process.

6. Feedback is especially useful for raising awareness of a problem and communicating expectations and potential repercussions of not solving it. A leader/coach may introduce a Performance Improvement Plan (PIP) in the feedback process, for example.

7. In Zone 1, the leader/coach doesn't necessarily have expertise in the area in which the team member/coachee requires assistance to solve their problem, but they often see the problem from a different vantage point. For example, their role in the company may allow them to see how the team member/coachee's problem is affecting the team, the company, or even the team member/coachee's future career with the company.

8. The leader/coach always determines the feedback topics.

9. During feedback, the team member/coachee always determines the action plan. Note that if the leader/coach introduces an action plan—within a PIP, for example—the team member/coachee enters a new coaching zone, such as training, mentoring, or collaboration, depending on the plan. At that point, feedback coaching ends, and the new coaching zone begins.

PART II QUESTIONS FOR REFLECTION

1. What feedback conversations do you need to have, or need to have more effectively, with your team?

2. What perceptions and behaviors might be hurting how others are perceiving your feedback?

3. How could you use feedback more effectively to drive better performance in others?

Part III

TRAINING

CHAPTER 8

Introduction to Zone 2: Training

Without training, they lacked knowledge. Without knowledge, they lacked confidence. Without confidence, they lacked victory.

—JULIUS CAESAR

Zone 2, training, is, "You have a problem. Here's how to fix it."

In this zone, a leader points out a problem and then strategically offers the coachee knowledge, tools, and resources to help them fix it.

Training is the transferring of knowledge, information, and skills so a person can perform an expected task.

Training is a great tool to use when someone doesn't have the knowledge required to fix a problem on their own. It's effective for filling in the gaps when they're missing concrete pieces of necessary knowledge.

THE GREAT TRAINING ROBBERY

In 2016, companies in the US spent over $70 billion on training and development programs.[1] Yet according to the Harvard Business School article, "Who Is to Blame for 'The Great Training Robbery'?" only 10 percent of corporate training is effective.[2]

This indicates that 90 percent of the money and time companies spend on training resources is wasted and does not help the bottom line. Why do companies continue to spend so much of their valuable resources on a tool that is not providing an efficient return on investment (ROI)?

As a training practitioner for over twenty years, I would argue that training gets a bad rap, but not because training is ineffective or fails to provide change. Rather, training is often set up to fail before it begins. It has become a corporate catchall for just about any people issues that arise within the organization. If a team member is underperforming, they're

---

1   "2016 Training Industry Report," *Training Magazine*, November/December 2016, accessed November 6, 2017, https://trainingmag.com/sites/default/files/images/Training_Industry_Report_2016.pdf.

2   Roberta Holland, "Who Is to Blame for 'The Great Training Robbery'?" *Harvard Business School Working Knowledge*, July 25, 2016, accessed November 6, 2017, https://hbswk.hbs.edu/item/whose-to-blame-for-the-great-training-robbery.

sent to training. If a new rollout of hardware, software, process, or protocol is needed, the answer is organization-wide training to catch everyone up to the changes. Whenever we need to get the next wave of high potentials ready for promotion, we send them to training.

Unfortunately, training is not the answer to every problem. The "Great Training Robbery" also states, "Too often CEOs turn to HR to create a training program when faced with a problem. The CEO avoids opening a Pandora's box of larger organizational flaws, and HR is happy to comply because it puts the function more at the center of things and avoids a risky conversation with the CEO about why training might not solve the problem."

Training is seen as the easy fix to problems, even when it isn't effective. Training is important, but to be effective, the right training must be used at the right time for the right kinds of issues.

It is important at this point to clarify our definition of training. As a reader, you may be viewing training in the formal sense of the word: a formalized live event with a clear agenda, curriculum, handout, or workbook, PowerPoint, and friendly facilitator from your Learning and Organizational Development Department. We need to broaden this view of training to help us see how to maximize this tool as a leader.

Our definition of training is the transferring of knowledge, information, and skills so a person can perform an expected task.

You already are a training coach. That may not be your title, and you may not report to HR, but if you are in a position of leadership, you are training people every day. You are driving results and instilling knowledge and skills to others as part of your leadership role.

Take a moment to reflect on that. By this definition, training is not only live events in a classroom but can include meetings, conference calls, workshops, webinars, eLearning, online videos, formalized live events, simulations, on-the-job instruction, monthly one-on-ones, and so much more. As you see from the many areas where training shows up, as a leader, you are probably doing a lot more training than you thought. You may not have the trainer title on your business card, yet you provide training. To say you are not a training coach because you don't work for the right department is equivalent to saying a parent isn't a teacher if they don't work in a school. The question isn't whether you're training people, but whether you are getting the results you want from the time you train others.

For example, most leaders have their fair share of meetings and conference calls with their people; however, how effective are these activities? Are people feeling empowered and able to perform their expected tasks better, or are these trainings just events that happen without true impact? Or worse, are these meetings causing people to feel more negative about their job and the organization? This can happen when we force people to attend live events or calls where they feel their time is wasted. Did you ever attend a meeting or a call where the organizer winged it without a formal agenda? People strayed off topic, and no one really brought the point around. No action items were passed along, and there was no follow-up.

All live events, virtual classes, and calls are not created equal. An effective leader understands there must be intent behind every agenda. A leader should ask themselves these two important questions:

- What does my audience need from me?
- What do I want from my audience?

Both are critical to the success of a training that leads to better performance.

We live in a corporate culture that focuses on only one of those questions. Unfortunately, it usually excludes what the learner needs or wants in the situation. If you realize that the point of most calls, meetings, formal workshops, and one-on-ones is transferring knowledge and skills to others, wouldn't you think considering what they want to get out of the event would be critical?

During every training moment you offer, whether formal or informal, the person being trained is asking one important question: "What's in it for me?" We call this the WIIFM.

CONSIDER YOUR AUDIENCE: BRYCE'S BLUNDER

Bryce was one of my directors early on in my career. When I joined his team, he provided me with some sage advice. He told me about the time he was trying to close a large deal with a new client. He had the client's team in for a meeting and a meal, and he went all out on the food and drinks. In an attempt to wow them, Bryce hired caterers to bring in a Brazilian barbeque. Servers would come to the table with knives and various quality cuts of meat speared on skewers. The client arrived, and Bryce was eager to find out what they thought of the incredible spread. He was told that while they appreciated the effort, the entire group was vegetarian.

Bryce prepared a meal he would have enjoyed if he were the client. Instead of asking them about their food preferences, he thought about what he wanted to provide. Can you imagine the message this sent to the potential client?

Leaders often treat training the same way. They think about how they want the meeting structured and what they want to say, but they fail to consider what works best for their audience.

This can lead to training failures, such as death by PowerPoint. Have you ever attended a training in which the presenter spent hours on slides, explaining each one in excruciating detail? This may work for a few select people in your audience, but little is retained, and many walk away feeling the presentation was not an effective use of their time. If the audience doesn't feel empowered and valued in the meeting, then what is the point?

FOUR PURPOSES OF TRAINING

Corporate trainers typically focus on the hard skills of training, basically, effective methods for developing and delivering training to a group. They have a defined objective, such as teaching a class of employees how to use a new piece of equipment or software application, or how to use a new process.

However, leaders—supervisors, managers, and executives, for example—who find themselves in training situations that arise throughout the day require certain soft skills to be effective.

No matter what type of training you are planning to deliver, there are four purposes that help you drive your intent behind the training: persuade, inspire, motivate, and challenge.

1. **Persuade**: Help people see the value of change and create compelling reasons to move forward. This often includes selling ideas or products.

2. **Inspire:** This focuses on creating commitment to new or established beliefs and values. It is more of an internal shift mentally and emotionally rather than a physical response.

3. **Motivate:** Move people to action. Act on old and new ways of thinking. The purpose here is to get the audience to double down on what they already know or to provide additional information that would help increase their buy-in to the idea.

4. **Challenge:** Present facts that challenge the group to think differently, often exploring both sides of an issue. This drives discussion and ideas that help create a shift in how people view a situation or product.

Did you notice one purpose that's missing? Leaders tend to think to "inform" is a specific reason to have a training, meeting, or call. Providing information is part of the purposes listed above. It is assumed in the content. However, it is a weak reason, by itself, to hold a training. What do you want the audience to do with the information you provide? When you designate a specific purpose and you understand what the people you are training want from the meeting as well, you will create an entirely different kind of training. This one shift will transform your impact as a leader. It drives the training format you select, how you organize the content, who is involved, and what follow-up will take place. It is the difference between putting a specific location into your GPS or simply driving around, hoping you'll find somewhere to go. Before you schedule training, ask yourself:

- What kinds of training are you currently providing (meetings, calls, one-on-ones, etc.)?
- Do you have a clear purpose in mind before you have a training?
- Do you understand the WIIFM of your team?
- What follow-up do you use to ensure people are using the information and tools effectively?
- How impactful are these events to the people attending them?

SELECTING THE RIGHT TRAINING FORMAT

Training environments, formats, venues, and delivery methods vary. Leaders have many in-person and virtual methods at their disposal to help participants learn key information and skills, and each one has its strengths and weaknesses. For this reason, leaders shouldn't get into a training rut with just one method but rather take a blended approach, choosing the right method for the training situation. In addition to using a variety of formats, you will get better results by combining methods. For example, follow a live training with materials for your students to read. Give them some practical examples that show them how they can apply what they've learned and give them an assignment that utilizes what they've learned. In this way, the people you're training will be more likely to grasp the training, remember it, and be able to use it in their work.

Here are four common training formats along with the pros and cons of each.

LIVE SESSIONS

Live sessions are those traditional, common training methods such as classroom events, live meetings, conference calls, live webinars, and workshops. The key component is a live training coach leads the event.

This training offers a spray approach to learning. There might be a standardized curriculum provided to the learners, and everyone goes through the same content regardless of their experience and skillset. This formal method may use adult learning methods to help integrate the content. For example, there may be activities, experiential learning questions, simulations, role-plays, assessments, and discussion groups. PowerPoint presentations and charts are often used to keep the visual learners stimulated, and there may be workbooks or handouts included.

Pros of Live Sessions

Live sessions build energy because a group of people receives training together in a closed room. This type of training reduces distractions that are typically hard to overcome in a normal work environment. By changing the surroundings, the leader changes the dynamic of the group and can provide a fresh perspective in how to approach the topic at hand.

Live sessions also ensure participants receive a consistent message. In theory, this training method jumpstarts the entire group of learners to move on a topic instead of relying on a trickle-down effect. Live sessions help address questions or concerns together, which provides an opportunity for more people to contribute to the discussion, creating a richer dialogue.

Cons of Live Sessions

Despite the pros, live sessions can have a low return on investment. This is because they tend to be overused and filled with live prisoners. Management might make attendance mandatory and force their people to attend without first gaining buy-in from them. It often becomes a show-up-and-check-the-box moment. This creates a hostage situation in which an already overworked team member now has something else to add to their list of things to do. Afterwards, they must make up for the time away from their actual work.

What makes the situation worse is that trainings and meetings are often poorly planned and executed. They lack a clear purpose. This means that many of the people attending are not only forced to be there, but they leave feeling as if little was accomplished.

CONFERENCE CALLS

Conference calls are a popular training method. They have the power to connect people without the bother and expense of bringing everyone together in the same room.

Pros of Conference Calls

This low-cost resource combines convenience with speed. It is a straightforward process to get everyone on a call to discuss urgent matters. Instead of coordinating different schedules and locations to bring the entire group together, conference calls allow everyone to jump on a call from their desk and talk through issues in real time. It is a cost-effective way to train team members. Leaders are now able to enhance simple calls with webinar and video tools that create a visual and impactful experience. The meetings can be recorded and offered to those on the team who were not able to attend the meeting live. PowerPoint and links can be integrated, offering options for visual and auditory learners. And with certain conference tools, there are breakout features that allow team members to discuss different items at the same time.

Cons of Conference Calls

There is an entire genre of humor around corporate conference call *faux pas*. From the one or two people forgetting to mute their lines to the constant beeps of people joining and exiting the calls, this style of training has many obstacles to overcome. It tends to be inexpensive and convenient, but the ROI is questionable in many cases. As participants multitask on other projects, the leader unloads a list of items to be covered. If the leader calls on a participant, we often hear the person silent for a moment as they try to get off mute and address the topic they were vaguely paying attention to. Conference calls require a lot more work to add the value you need to make them meaningful.

ON-THE-JOB TRAINING

On-the-job training is when team members learn to perform tasks and skills in the real world. They observe leaders and/

or peers and then practice the skills. This type of training is more targeted toward the individual learner and focuses on specific, job-related activities.

Pros of On-The-Job Training

On-the-job training saves time since it meets the learner where they are in their job and in their work. It doesn't follow a page-by-page curriculum but spends needed time on the critical areas of understanding that the learner has. Since it is provided live in the real work environment, practice tends to be with real cases and customers. This creates more of an immersion learning technique than a textbook style of learning, like the difference between learning Spanish in a high school classroom and learning the language by moving to Mexico and attending a school where everyone speaks Spanish.

On-the-job training experts provide hacks and shortcuts to systems. The learner gets the answers to their questions as they come up, and they are addressed immediately. Knowledge tends to stick more, since it is cerebral in nature. This means muscle memory is created by doing the actual work while it is being learned.

Cons of On-The-Job Training

On-the-job training is only as effective as the leader or person providing the training. If the leader is a poor teacher, then many items the person who's being trained needs to know may be left out. Just because a top sales person can deliver exceptional results doesn't mean they know how to pass along that skill to others in a way that helps them create the same behaviors. Some educators call this quality "unconscious competence," where the expert is not sure why they are successful, but they have learned to do things well. An effective leader knows what needs to be taught and how to teach it, and they know how to break things down in teachable steps that help the learner gain the skills needed.

Since there are limited standard reading materials associated with on-the-job training, inconsistency is common. One on-the-job training may be thorough and complete, or it may provide the individual with little information. This makes holding the individual accountable difficult since there was no standard training or content that covered all the required skills and knowledge. Another issue is that critical legal and HR topics may be excluded from the training, which can later come back to haunt the organization in lawsuits and customer escalations.

VIRTUAL TRAINING

Virtual training is becoming more popular and includes eLearning, virtual on-demand training, online books, articles, and abstracts, microlearning, and recorded webinars.

If your organization is large enough, you probably have a Learning Management System (LMS) full of virtual learning opportunities.

Pros of Virtual Training

Although eLearning and virtual on-demand classes are not cheap, they can be cost-effective over the long term compared to live session training. While flying a trainer in and having everyone drop what they're doing for a day or two of live training can affect productivity and be expensive, eLearning classes can save time and resources by providing courses for team members to complete when it is convenient. That way, people can plan their trainings around big projects or critical deadlines.

Microlearning is the latest fad, with three-to-five-minute videos that cover a variety of topics. Instead of spending hours on a specific topic, you can learn core competencies in a few minutes and practice them immediately. Then you can come back and learn something else when you have time and are ready to practice.

Abstracts have renewed people's appetite for reading. Instead of spending hours and days reading a trending business book, you can check out companies like Books24x7 and getAbstract, which offer five-page summaries of core concepts from these books. This method of training saves leaders and individuals a lot of time and provides the knowledge needed for growth and development.

Cons of Virtual Training

Virtual alternatives provide profound knowledge around hard skills training classes, the learning that is less subjective and more concrete. For example, it's an effective way to train people to master spreadsheet techniques. Virtual learning solutions become less effective with soft-skills training. Leadership development, management skills, sales, and customer service training are difficult without a leader to provide reflection and awareness on what the participant needs to work on specifically. By the same token, watching someone model selling behaviors doesn't guarantee I will be able to go out and perform the same behaviors.

Now that you understand the four most common training formats, let's talk about how you can apply them more effectively.

CHAPTER 9

MOR: A Better Way to Train

Leadership and learning are indispensable to each other.

—JOHN F. KENNEDY

Traditionally, when leaders provide training, they focus on what they're going to train, when they're going to train it, and where they're going to train. Those are important considerations, but even more importantly, leaders need to focus on motivation, ownership, and real-world application (MOR).

The MOR process focuses on why, who, and how. The why, who, and how are arguably more important than the what, when, and where.

I'm not suggesting you take on anything new, but simply enhance what you're already doing by looking at training from a unique perspective and focusing on these critical questions—the why, the who, and the how.

MOTIVATION

As we discussed earlier, when faced with training, people ask themselves, "What's in it for me? What problems will this training help solve, and how does this apply to my world?"

Clear answers to these questions are key to providing your team with proper motivation. To be effective, training must be relevant to real-life problems and tasks, and it must boost your team members' performance levels and make something in their lives better and more satisfying in some way.

There is an assumption that everyone wants to grow and develop. Unfortunately, this just isn't the case. Adult learners tend to do what they're rewarded for, so if a leader or organization does not reward growth, people may not instigate development. They'll do whatever gets them a promotion or more money. They may even join a company with a robust development program just because it offers them potential growth options, but many of these same people fail to ever take the classes or sign up for personal development if it is not required.

One organization I joined had a large development program. They spent over fifty thousand dollars on virtual on-demand classes from one national vendor alone. As I considered how many people were taking advantage of these courses, I learned that in two years only fifteen people had ever taken classes, and most of those were in a leadership program that required it. There were about five people voluntarily working on specific growth opportunities not tied to mandatory programs. Fifty thousand dollars was a large price to pay for a handful of people.

As a leader, part of your coaching role is to ensure the people you're training have a clear motivation for changing. Help them understand how the training ties into the bigger picture and how it will get them where they want to go. Essentially, you must establish the reward. Sometimes that might be monetary, and sometimes it's something else.

This isn't to say monetary gains are the best way to reward development, but people need a reason to participate in training. People do things for a purpose when they're motivated by distinct reasons. As a leader, your job is to make sure you're tying whatever you're trying to teach to a motivation—you must speak the language of the people going through the training.

OWNERSHIP

Depending on the kind of training you provide, you can't always allow flexibility and ownership. For example, if you're teaching someone to use a machine that runs a certain way, perhaps where buttons and levers must be activated in a particular order, you might have to teach that a specific way. But for most trainings, leaders can help people own their learning experience.

You can provide your team with opportunities for ownership by providing choices. For example, you can tell them the topics you need to cover and ask them which one they want to explore right now. This gives them some control over the experience.

LEARNING STRATEGIES

You can also offer diverse ways to learn the content. Learning strategies are tactics that have been scientifically tested and proven to increase learning and retention. The three trending methods are distributed, interleaved, and retrieval. Here is an overly simplified summary of each.

Distributed learning is when each learning session is broken down into shorter periods of time and then provided more frequently. Many learners are experiencing short-term success by cramming longer periods of time on one subject, but they are not retaining the content long term. Individuals who learn in shorter sessions over a longer period are able to retain and absorb the material for a greater period of time.[1]

---

1   "Distributed practice," *Wikipedia*, edited October 25, 2017, accessed March 25, 2018, https://en.wikipedia.org/wiki/Distributed_practice.

The Interleaved method takes similar topics that can build on each other. For example, if you want to learn to play tennis, the traditional approach might be to work on your backhand for hours and hours until you have mastered that one skill and then move on to the next skill. In this method, an example might include a regiment of ten minutes on serving, then ten minutes on backhand, followed by ten minutes of running, and ending with ten minutes of stretches. They are short periods of time that build on each other. By shortening the skill practice and doing other skills that are related, it brings the individual skills and the entire performance up faster than just focusing on one area. Studies have found that by doing it this way, learners will retain 10 percent more information when they space their learning than when they study the same information in longer blocks.[2]

The Retrieval method is a practice testing method in which you provide a practice test that assesses the learner's current knowledge (the information in their head). Then you evaluate what they really know about the subject. The secret to this method is to evaluate what is truly within their understanding versus what they are guessing and happen to get right by sheer chance. It helps them evaluate how they are learning and whether it is effective or needs to be adjusted before they have the real exam or evaluation. This method

2   Marianne Stenger, "Interleaved Practice: 4 Ways to Learn Better by Mixing It Up," *InformED*, September 9, 2016, accessed March 25, 2018, https://www.opencolleges.edu.au/informed/learning-strategies/interleaved-practice-4-ways-to-learn-better-by-mixing-it-up.

provides a rehearsal or practice environment instead of simply building up to one test or performance evaluation.[3]

LEARNING STYLES

Learning styles provide additional tools to help individuals absorb content in more efficient ways. The three most common learning styles are visual, auditory, and kinesthetic. Although some scholars debate the impact of using learning styles when training, I personally believe they are worth considering when enhancing the learning environment. As with all adult learning methods, I wouldn't recommend taking any one technique or tactic to an extreme.

Visual Learners

First are visual learners. They like graphs, charts, and pictures. They want to see the concepts, not just hear about them. They like clear instructions written out and materials they can read.

Auditory Learners

Second are auditory learners. These people tend to not care about visuals in the room and prefer someone talk through

---

3   "Promoting Metacognition with Retrieval Practice in Five Steps," *The Effortful Educator*, April 3, 2017, accessed March 25, 2018, https://theeffortfuleducator.com/2017/04/03/promoting-metacognition-with-retrieval-practice-in-five-steps.

the materials. Don't ask auditory learners to read things to themselves, but plan on talking things out with them. They prefer engaging presenters who have stories to tell. They like music in the room to listen to when presenters are not leading the discussion. They prefer verbal instructions and discussion groups to talk about key points.

Kinesthetic Learners

Third, kinesthetic learners are the hands-on folks in the group. They want to be exploring the concepts with activities. They need something to do instead of sitting and listening or watching someone else lead. These folks will often need something in their hands to play with, and they gravitate toward activities that get them up and moving around. They will multitask and fidget with whatever is in their hands. The fidget-spinner industry emerged from this group of learners. They learn by being in motion.

Learning Styles Example: Car Shopping

Here's an illustration of these learning styles. Imagine you're selling cars at a dealership, and each one of these folks came in to look around your lot. The visual learner would probably walk up to the cars and read the stickers. They would gravitate toward any brochures and signs they could read. They would want to look over the car manual and other resources to help them make a buying decision. On the flip side, the auditory learner would go looking for someone to talk to. They would want to ask questions and hear about the car features from an expert. The last person, the kinesthetic learner, would skip the materials and person altogether. They would want to sit in the car, smell the new car smell, and play with the buttons and features. They would want to take a test drive!

If a sales person only sold one way and failed to adapt their style to the learner, you can see how it would limit their ability to close sales. If a leader or whoever provides the training is auditory, they tend to talk everything out. But people in the room with other learning styles would struggle with the lack of visuals and activities. The same is true for a visual leader who wants to provide a lot of graphs and charts but does not provide engaging discussions and activities. Providing a balanced, blended, training environment with your learners in mind will enhance the learning potential and allow more ownership for people in the room. If your training is a meeting or one-on-one, then adapt your style to the person you are speaking with.

Training sometimes follows the shotgun approach, in which leaders spray people with ideas and hope some of them stick. They throw all the information and tools at their people and think they've done their due diligence. People don't learn much if anything from these information dumps. They implement very few of the tools and can't do what is asked of them. It's like trying to take a drink from a fire hydrant—you get wet, but you don't get much to drink.

When you give people control over their learning experience, they can move at their own pace and in the directions that make sense to them, and thus, they learn more effectively. Don't force your people to learn something. Allow them to become part of the learning process.

If someone told me to research all those topics, I would have been resistant, but when given the opportunity to explore, I became much more invested in the topic and made the extra effort to learn. I might be reading a book and based on the author's recommendation, I would follow-up with another book, article, or YouTube video that provided more information.

Unfortunately, leaders tend to micromanage the learning process. They have the attitude, "I want you to know exactly what I want you to know. Here's your checklist. Go through these items and then take a test to prove you know what I want you to know." Again, training doesn't have to be a pass-or-fail learning event. It can be a learning journey. Learning journeys occur when you give your team members choices and control, allowing them to take ownership and to choose the knowledge they want. Even when you teach black-and-white topics, you can still provide choices and create ownership. The ultimate impact in learning happens when learners become the teachers themselves. This provides the highest retention for the individual.

There is an illustration of a grumpy little kid with his arms crossed, saying, "I may be sitting down on the outside, but I'm standing up on the inside." That's what this issue comes down to. People who don't have ownership in their training experience might be sitting down on the outside but standing up on the inside. As a leader, you might think you're in control of the people you're training, but you're not. The only thing you're in control of is your ability to invite those people to learn and grow.

LETTING GO

Letting go of control can be tough for leaders, even profes-sional facilitators. It's tough because we think the fastest way to get somewhere is to have that control: just command it to be done, and it's done. But training needs to be more of a partnership than a top-down dictation. When you take on the role of training coach, your job is to invite each person to create their own experience out of the coaching.

The goal of training is to transfer knowledge to improve performance. This ultimately leads to better results. If you don't train people in a way that creates a partnership, they won't be open to learning, and they definitely won't be open to applying the information. They'll feel an inner resistance to accepting it and will never create the change necessary to drive better results.

Training isn't about knowing all the greatest training techniques. The key to training is understanding that the people you are training are the ones in control, and your job is to give them ownership of the process and then help them develop through partnership.

REAL-WORLD APPLICATION

Real-world application refers to training applied to real-life scenarios and not just providing content. This keeps the training real. There must be a purpose and an application for the training.

In one organization I worked for, the ramp-up time for new employees was incredibly long because the training wasn't being implemented effectively. In fact, managers would often say, "Go to training, learn what you can, but when you get back, we'll talk about what you really need to do." Training needs to have real-world applications so people can put it into practice. Training must have a relevance factor, be directly tied to what people need to do for their jobs and teach the skills they use in their day-to-day job duties.

We often think people are learning when we give them information, but they're really learning when they apply the information. As a result, effective training makes use of real-world stories, examples, and illustrations. Simulations, case studies, role playing, and on-the-job training are great tools that help the learning process. These tools not only reveal whether participants understand the material but also allow them to put the training into action in a comfortable way.

LETTING GO: LONDON'S LESSON

As an example, I was teaching my oldest son, London, how to mow the lawn. My yard is important to me. I see it as a statement to the neighborhood, so I work hard to take care of it. I make sure the lines are perfect when I mow, and I have a certain method for going around bushes with the mower. (Yes, I realize that in the big scheme of things, my lawn really isn't that important. Understand, my ego is at stake here, and I'm pretty sure I'm not the only homeowner who feels this way about their lawn.)

Entrusting this care to my twelve-year-old son was difficult for me, but the time had come for me to teach him the art of mowing grass.

Outside, I wanted to teach my son about the lawn mower, but he said, "I don't need to know about the lawn mower. I know how to start it, Dad. I know how to do this."

"No, no," I said. "We need to talk about the lawn mower. We need to talk about how it works and about the lines and patterns and how to go around obstacles."

"No, I got this," he said. "I got this."

I could have told my son to sit on the sidewalk and watch me, and then do what I did. That's what I wanted to do because I thought it was the best way for him to learn. But then I recognized that I had to let him take control of owning this experience. I wanted to talk him through everything to try to prevent him from having problems. But what if I just hung around instead, and if he got stuck, help him? That approach was less about preventing problems and more about being present to help with problems that arose through my son's own learning process. By letting him try things his way, he could have both ownership and real-world application in the learning experience.

So, I said, "All right, you got it. Take off."

He started mowing, and then he stopped. Each time he got stuck, he asked, "What do I do here?"

At that point, he was open to dialogue, but if I had forced the dialogue on him beforehand and dumped all the details on him, he wouldn't have listened.

When my son was done mowing, I said, "Okay, let's walk through and look at your work."

He'd done well in some places, but there were also huge

sections of tall grass that he'd missed. He'd been trying to get done so quickly that the quality had suffered.

"This is a great start," I said. "Now, is there anything you might need to do differently here?"

He looked at the tall grass and said, "I may need to fix a few spots."

"Sounds good. Why don't you go ahead and fix those spots?"

If I had simply mowed the lawn myself, it would have been done faster and better, but that wasn't the point. The point was to teach him how to do it. And if I had forced all the information about my process on him, he might not have missed so many spots and had to do it over again, but that also wasn't the point. It was about partnering with him and letting him explore the ways to mow. That kept the process real for him, and he learned more from his mistakes than he would have from me talking at him. Learning from mistakes is a large part of how people learn and another reason why training has to be real.

PART III CONCLUSION

Before your next training session, review the MOR process—motivation, ownership, and real-world application—which comprise principles and not steps. Gear your training toward the MOR principles in whatever way makes sense for your team.

Take some time to reflect on what you can do to be a better training coach. Ask yourself these questions:

1. How am I currently training?
2. What's missing from my ability to become a great training coach?
3. What do I need to own in this process?
4. What do I need to work on in the MOR process?
5. What do I need to do to create motivation?
6. What do I need to do to give my people ownership over their learning process?
7. What can I do to integrate these learning processes into our real-world, day-to-day work and make sure the training is implemented?
8. What am I doing to make sure this is a learning journey, not a learning event?
9. What can I do from my role even when I'm not an expert in that field?

There's no reason to be overwhelmed by training. It's simple if you focus on the MOR principles. When you discover the answers to the previous questions, then you can start becoming a better training coach.

WHAT IS TRAINING?

1. Training is the transferring of knowledge, information, and skills so a person can perform an expected task.

2. Training is initiated when a leader/coach essentially says, "You have a problem. Here's how to fix it."

3. In Zone 2, training, the team member/coachee may or may not be aware of the coaching need. While they may be aware there is a gap in their learning, they are usually unaware of the extent of their lack of knowledge. In other words, they don't know what they don't know.

4. Training is an effective coaching tool when a team member doesn't have the knowledge required to fix a problem on their own.

5. The leader/coach points out a problem and then strategically offers knowledge, tools, and resources to team members to help them fix it through the training process.

6. Training fills in the gaps when a team member/coachee is missing concrete pieces of necessary knowledge.

7. In Zone 2, the leader/coach does not have to be an expert in the field in which they are coaching, but they should have enough knowledge to be able to offer useful training that satisfies the needs of the team member/coachee.

8. The leader/coach determines the training topics. The team member/coachee may do some research and identify potential training courses, but it is the leader who ultimately determines or approves the topics required to satisfy the team member's needs.

9. During the training process, the team member/coachee also determines the action plan, although again, the team member may initially research potential training-plan options. These options may involve other coaching zones, such as mentoring or collaboration.

PART III QUESTIONS FOR REFLECTION

1. How can you as a leader provide MOR when training your team members?

2. Why is it so important to identify the WIIFM when presenting content of any kind to others?

3. How can you turn simple meetings and calls into meaningful training moments for those who are participating?

Part IV

MENTORING

CHAPTER 10

Introduction to Zone 3: Mentoring

The delicate balance of mentoring someone is not creating them in your own image, but giving them the opportunity to create themselves.

—STEVEN SPIELBERG

Zone 3, mentoring, marks a shift in awareness. Instead of the leader bringing the problem to the team member's attention, the team member approaches the leader with the issue: "I have a problem. Fix me."

Mentoring is the process where two individuals enter into a learning relationship together that has focused objectives, established boundaries, and a clear timeline.

Mentoring is different from training because, while a training coach doesn't have to be an expert in the field they train, a mentor does. In Zone 3, a mentor must come from a wealth of experience and extensive knowledge in the area they're coaching. They can guide others through problems because they've been there and done that.

In the foreword to *The Mentor's Guide,* Lois J. Zachary provides this metaphor for mentorship:

> Ecologists tell us that a tree planted in the clearing of an old forest will grow more successfully than one planted in an open field. The reason, it seems, is that the roots of the forest tree are able to follow the intricate pathways created by former trees and thus embed themselves more deeply. Indeed, over time, the roots of many trees may actually grasp themselves to one another, creating an interdependent mat of life hidden beneath the earth. This literally enables the stronger trees to share resources with the weaker ones so the whole forest becomes healthier.[1]

I love this example because it emphasizes how mentors are people who have paved the way to help others do great things.

But where does mentoring fit within coaching? While the coaching zones aren't steps, one may naturally lead to

---

1   Lois J. Zachary, *The Mentor's Guide: Facilitating Effective Learning Relationships*, 2nd ed. (San Francisco: Jossey-Bass, 2011).

another. This is common between training and mentoring. Although they are related coaching methods, there are distinct differences at their core.

TRAINING VS. MENTORING

Highly effective leaders who provide training to their people as part of their supervisory or managerial roles have a few things in common. First, they understand training principles that allow them to optimize teachable moments for participants. Second, they don't have to be experts in the area they are training. Good leaders as training coaches can use the same adult learning principles and apply them to just about any subject. Their expertise is the training process, not necessarily the content. There are leaders who have both training skills and deep knowledge in a subject, but that is not required to be a successful trainer. The important thing to remember is that a training coach uses learned principles to communicate knowledge and skills.

Mentoring, on the other hand, typically occurs between two individuals in a one-on-one format. There are exceptions, which we will discuss later. The leader as mentor has a unique skillset and experience that the team member is looking to obtain. In this relationship, the mentor is usually an expert, or at least more advanced in their ability to perform a task. For example, consider if you were having legal trouble and being sued. Although there are people in your life who could provide advice, it would probably make more sense to consult with an attorney. This expert would advise you differently than someone who is offering you an uneducated opinion. In this case, the attorney would become a mentor for you.

The same is true concerning your taxes. There are those who can provide tax support about how to enter your information into TurboTax, the online tax program. However, having a seasoned CPA guide you through the tax laws and implications of the tax codes can provide a totally unique perspective. Mentors do just that. In many cases, they have been down the road you are about to walk. They can tell you the challenges you may face and the rewards you could expect to experience by taking this next step.

To help us distinguish this unique form of coaching, let's review our definition: Mentoring is the process where two individuals enter into a learning relationship together that has focused objectives, established boundaries, and a clear timeline.

Although there are many definitions of mentoring and mentorships that would color outside the lines of the one I offer here, based on my experience, this definition provides a formula for the best results from this type of coaching relationship.

Mentorship is the zone where self-awareness shifts. In Zone 1, the stimulus that initiated the coaching was "You have a problem. Go fix it," and in Zone 2, it was "You have a problem. Here's how you fix it." In Zone 3, the team member says, "I have a problem. Fix me." The team member, not the manager, has identified a problem and is seeking help.

Mentorships are most effective when the team member seeks out a mentor. If a manager tells them, "You need my help. Let me mentor you," or if there's a program set up where everyone gets a preassigned mentor, the impact of the mentor relationship may be limited.

With a mentorship relationship, the team member goes to an expert for specific advice. If you go to your doctor with chest pains, you want him or her to diagnose you with something so the two of you can work to fix the chest pains. In this case, you are not asking for training, but rather for a relationship with an expert who can assist you with a specific question, advice, or skill.

MENTORING ESSENTIALS

Mentorship is not just about providing an expert opinion. There are certain skills that a mentor develops to maximize the time they spend and their relationship with the mentee. Following are seven vital qualities in a mentor relationship.

ESSENTIAL #1: DEVELOPING RAPPORT

One-sided relationships can shut down rapport between two people. The secret to building rapport is based, primarily, on an appropriate amount of give and take. Using active listening skills helps jumpstart the trust and safety between the mentor and mentee. Following are some active listening skill basics:

- Eye contact
- Facial expression
- Tone, gestures
- Posture
- Responsive listening
- "I" statements
- Being authentic and sincere
- Verifying and paraphrasing

ESSENTIAL #2: SEEKING FACTS

Rather than taking a cursory interest in the person you're mentoring, you must engage with them to build a solid mentor relationship. Learn the facts of their situation and seek to understand their world, perspective, and background. You can do this by simply asking questions.

ESSENTIAL #3: ASKING QUESTIONS

Using open-ended questions can draw out the mentee's

assumptions. Questions stimulate thinking in a way that advice can never do. We will let a powerful question penetrate our thinking and feelings, but when that same information is packaged in the form of advice and opinions, we are much more guarded about letting the information in. Using hypothetical questions can also help bring down the walls and help the mentee explore new ways of thinking about a situation from a safe place.

ESSENTIAL #4: CHALLENGING THINKING AND BEHAVIOR

A good mentor not only listens but also knows when to speak up and challenge the mentee's thinking and behaviors. Some people seek out a mentor relationship to justify their decisions or way of thinking. The mentor should be prepared for this and ready and willing to provide appropriate feedback. By challenging ideas and behaviors, the mentor helps the mentee assess why they hold certain beliefs and helps them decide whether they want to continue to do so.

ESSENTIAL #5: MODELING

The mentor usually comes into the relationship with a wealth of knowledge and experience. They have examples and stories that can help the mentee see potential obstacles ahead. They know hacks and shortcuts that can save time. The mentor has successes and failures to draw from and help the mentee learn from, so they can avoid the same mistakes and get to their desired goal faster. In many cases, with this experience comes humility and wisdom. Wise mentors have had to battle their own egos and face their own insecurities. They clearly see their own shortcomings, qualities often lacking by people just beginning the process. By modeling these behaviors, they teach the mentee to approach the situation authentically and with a touch of humanity.

ESSENTIAL #6: SHARED GROWTH

Although people tend to view mentors as the only person in the mentor-mentee relationship with broad experience and knowledge, the best mentor relationships develop when the mentor is also learning and growing. This development may be in very different areas than the subjects on which they are mentoring. The key is that the mentor relationship can and should be an opportunity for both people to stretch their own skills and understanding. In some cases, the mentor may learn more from the mentee than the mentee learns from them. It is important that both people approach the relationship with the opportunity to grow and change.

ESSENTIAL #7: CREATING CHANGE

The mentor relationship should lead toward change. As the mentee sets certain goals and targets for themselves, the mentor partners with them to pursue those goals together.

The mentor affirms positive steps forward and challenges the mentee when they hit obstacles or walls. The mentor helps course correct and clarify as they progress. They help provide encouragement that the mentee is not alone in the process but has a guide with whom to walk the learning journey.

SEVEN ESSENTIALS OF MENTORING

These seven essential skills will maximize the time spent between a mentor and mentee.

- **Mentoring Essential #1**: Developing rapport.

- **Mentoring Essential #2**: Seeking facts.

- **Mentoring Essential #3**: Asking questions.

- **Mentoring Essential #4**: Challenged thinking and behavior.

- **Mentoring Essential #5**: Modeling.

- **Mentoring Essential #6**: Shared growth.

- **Mentoring Essential #7**: Creating change.

MISGUIDED MENTORSHIPS: FELIPE'S FAUX PAS

Felipe was an IT specialist at a large corporation. He was well-known around the company, but not for the right reasons. His knowledge of the network was second to none, and people saw him as intelligent and talented. However, his people skills were sorely lacking. Felipe fixed problems others would miss, but his blunt and often abrasive communication style made people avoid him. Felipe wanted to progress in his career and move into a management position, but he kept getting passed up for these roles, which went to less talented, less experienced individuals. Frustrated, Felipe asked a human resources VP to mentor him.

What seemed obvious to everyone else—Felipe's abrasiveness—wasn't obvious to him. His lack of self-awareness made identifying gaps and setting goals difficult in each mentoring session. Felipe complained about being treated unfairly, and he missed the point of the mentorship: working on himself and his behaviors. Although his mentor tried to guide the conversations back to the core issues, little progress was made. Felipe failed to take advantage of the mentoring to elevate his status, and his behaviors continued to hurt his relationships. At the next round of IT cutbacks, he lost his job.

Many mentor relationships fail before they ever begin. It's not uncommon to have a team member approach a potential mentor and say, "Okay, fix me," without having any specific issues to address in mind or being open to learning what they may be. That would be like going to the doctor and saying, "I want to be the healthiest person alive. Fix me." In the fifteen minutes the doctor has for your appointment, he or she isn't going to be able to completely fix everything about your health.

Some people think mentorship is informal and focused on

mentoring an entire person. They see mentorship as finding someone they admire and respect and then spending a lot of time with that person: following them around, having general discussions with them, going to lunch, and so on. Using our previous doctor analogy, that would be like going back to your doctor without any real reason to be there and saying, "Hey, why don't we just kind of talk? I'll follow you around a little bit, and maybe you can diagnose me along the way." It doesn't work like that with doctors or with mentors. When you're not specific about the goals of the mentorship, it's easy to get in a situation where you're just having a friendly conversation over a cup of coffee and building a relationship. There's nothing wrong with that, but it's not mentorship.

MENTORING DIRECT REPORTS

As a leader, it is important to remember that mentoring direct reports can be difficult at times but not impossible. For example, if one of your direct reports wants to explore growth opportunities outside of your department and this person is critical to your team, you may attempt to persuade them otherwise, even though this may be a good career move for them. Self-awareness on your part as the leader is key to mentoring someone who affects your results and metrics. Just think how you would feel if your doctor prescribed a medicine that he or she received a financial kickback for every time a patient bought it. This would harm your trust of the doctor and your view of their medical opinion. If you are not able to offer a clear and unbiased mentor relationship, you may want to refer the individual to other leaders who can be more objective with your team member.

AVOIDING THE MINI-ME

People often gravitate toward mentors who are just like them, but the ideal mentor has a different perspective than you, so they can help you grow and see things you don't see in yourself. When you pick a mentor who is just like you, it's easy to fall into the trap of hearing only what you want to hear. Then you'll continue seeing the world as you've always seen it. Sometimes people even look at mentors as justifications for why they can continue doing what they want to do instead of growing and changing. It's easy to talk to someone if they're telling us what we want to hear, but a great mentor is someone who's willing to speak the truth and tell you what you need to hear.

HELPING YOUR PEOPLE FIND MENTORS

Sometimes you may be the mentor, but part of your job, as leader, will also be to help your team members navigate Zone 3 with other mentors. If that's the case, first help your team member determine how to pick a mentor. I'll get into the traits of what makes a good mentor soon, but one of the most important considerations when choosing a mentor is identifying someone who will help you truly grow and not just someone who is convenient.

CHAPTER 11

Mentorship
Agreements

A mentor is someone who sees more talent and ability within you,
than you see in yourself, and helps bring it out of you.

—BOB PROCTOR

The best mentorships are focused and organized. Leaders simply don't have time to mentor all aspects of an individual's work and life, and the higher a person goes in leadership, the less time they must invest in a good conversation. Mentorships need to focus on something specific, like a certain project or skill. An agreement, formal or informal, is made between mentor and mentee to focus on specific issues, and then you mentor to that agreement. There needs to be a clearly defined relationship with set parameters, a clear goal, and an action plan to achieve the goal. Mentorships lead toward some element of change—something the team member is working on—so they can produce better results, better relationships, or improvements of some kind.

THE MENTORSHIP AGREEMENT: BILL AND TED'S EXCELLENT EXPERIENCE

Bill has a time management problem and can't seem to find time to attend training to fix the problem. Instead, he finds an expert in the organization's leadership, Ted, who's skilled at time management, and asks for help.

"Ted," says Bill, "I need help with time management and would like you to mentor me."

"All right," says Ted. "What will our mentoring relationship look like?"

Bill replies, "I'd like us to spend some time going through my day-to-day processes. Maybe you can give me guidance based on what you do to address similar situations. You might also suggest some books or recommend an online class I could take—whatever you think might help me. Then we can follow up in a week and see if I'm making progress."

Ted agrees.

In this example, Bill and Ted agree to a certain process and timeline. They agree to what they're going to do and when

this mentorship will end. Instead of having an ongoing, neb-
ulous, long-term mentorship, they've established clear goals
and expectations for what the mentorship should provide.
Mentoring is a powerful tool, but it is critical to establish
clear boundaries and timelines.

Sometimes other issues come up in a mentorship. You may
have contracted to work on one element, but another gap
comes up, and you agree to address that too. If you have
the expertise and availability, then adjust the goals, process,
and timeline, and continue mentoring, but remember that
you are not mentoring the entire person. You are addressing needs.

By focusing on specific needs instead of entire people, you
can avoid catchall mentorships. Remember that mentors
must be experts in the subject matter, so mentorships that
try to fix entire people rarely work. Just because someone
is an expert at accounting doesn't mean you want them
operating on you in surgery. If someone has multiple issues,
they might be better off having three different mentors who
are experts in each one of those individual areas instead
of one person who might be great at one and so-so at the
other two. Mentoring toward one skill instead of trying to
fix a whole person allows the mentee to provide the best
help possible.

CREATING MENTORSHIP AGREEMENTS

Mentorship agreements include both formal and informal commitments between the mentor and mentee. I wouldn't go as far as using the word "contract;" however, these agreements define the relationship and how both parties will approach their role in it.

You may be wondering why you would need to be so formal in this relationship. I would say it depends on the situation. In some cases, you wouldn't. But in many cases, a well-defined mentorship role will help you optimize the experience. It helps the mentee articulate what they want and the mentor to articulate what they can provide. This clarity propels the relationship forward. It not only helps establish specific targets and goals but, more importantly, measurements to determine if those goals were reached and how they are going to be reached. Think of it in terms of the difference in saying, "At some point tonight, let's get in the car and drive around until we find a place to eat dinner," versus "Let's head downtown to the Cheesecake Factory and eat dinner at 6:00 p.m." Both statements will lead to getting something to eat, yet the experience of how you get there and what happens along the way will be totally different.

WHAT IS INCLUDED IN A MENTOR AGREEMENT?

Three core components comprise a mentor agreement: gap assessment, goal statement, and game plan.

- **Gap Assessment**: The gap description and assessment help identify what is missing and needs to be addressed. This is a fact-finding mission to get as much relevant information as possible to understand what is causing the problem.
- **Goal Statement**: The goal statement describes where the mentee wants to ultimately end up.
- **Game Plan**: The game plan is composed of the steps and processes that need to take place to achieve the goal.

Refer to Chapter 17, "The Coach's Playbook," for more on creating a mentorship agreement.

THE MENTOR AGREEMENT IN ACTION: SEAN'S SHUFFLE

Sean, a VP of HR, received some bad news on the employees' internal, quarterly engagement assessment. The latest scores revealed engagement scores had dropped by more than twelve percentage points. This was alarming. The feedback from the surveys revealed that team members felt managers were not listening to their concerns or invested in their personal development. Sean needed to fix the problem quickly before it caused bigger problems within the organization.

Using Sean's situation as an example, take a moment to answer these questions and practice your mentor skills:

What is the **Problem**?

....

What is the **Gap**?

....

What is the **Goal**?

....

What is the **Game Plan**?

....

We need more information before we can help Sean and his team. Let's walk through some of the questions I asked Sean in our mentoring session.

"Sean, I can see why you would be concerned by this situation. Let's begin with the end in mind. What is the ideal goal for you and your organization concerning these issues?"

He responded, "We need to have our team engagement scores at eighty-five percent by the end of the year."

"Sean, what would hitting eighty-five percent do for you and the organization?"

"We believe it makes happier employees, and that will make people want to stay longer. Not to mention this metric is tied to our yearly company bonus."

"So if I understand correctly, you want higher engagement scores because it makes people happier and they want to stay longer. Also, your bonus is based on these scores as well."

He responded, "Yes."

"It sounds like more people are leaving than you would like. What is causing your high turnover within the organization?"

"We are extremely focused on cost efficiencies. We have been in the process of cutting costs for the last five years. Our stakeholders see us as a leader in cost efficiencies among our competitors in the same industry. This means people need to do more with less. Because of this, there has been limited time to develop our people or our bench strength for internal promotions. People are being promoted before they are ready. This is creating bigger problems in the long run."

Now we have a lot more to go on to answer those questions. First, there is the whole matter of Sean being worried about not getting paid his bonus based on these engagement scores.

I think his company had good intentions by tying an important metric to a financial incentive. This approach often happens in sales and customer service groups concerning customer satisfaction scores (CSAT).

Although financial incentives drive awareness and results to any focus area, you run the risk of employees manipulating feedback so they get paid. There is a great debate among leaders about what produces exceptional customer satisfaction and employee engagement. Paying bonuses and commissions directly related to satisfaction and engagement can come across as buying positive responses, which can mask larger problems. When a single negative comment—whether that of the customer or of the employee—takes money out of the employee's pocket, the truth can get skewed. The other side of the argument is that it means people will focus on providing exceptional customer service if their bonus or salary is connected. We could spend several chapters of this book on these different schools of thinking. However, I will just say that the best engagement and customer satisfaction comes from truly happy team members. Companies can manipulate and drive results from fear and incentives, but the long-term solution is creating a culture that is authentically invested in their people.

Next, we have learned that the company goal was less about hitting new revenue markers and more about focusing on reducing costs and overhead. This changes the way Sean will want to set up his goal. As we talked further, it became apparent that his organization often talked about their number one goal being driving revenue. However, the evidence was to the contrary. They spent their energy and focus on running lean and efficient. This was evident in the yearly layoffs and cutbacks the employees came to expect. It caused fear throughout the entire organization during certain times of the year. Employees felt there was little loyalty to them and that they were expendable. Sean would later realize this would have an impact on engagement and turnover.

Now that we have more information, let's try this again. We need to identify the problem and the gap assessment, goal statement, and game plan so we can set up an initial mentorship agreement.

Problem: Employee engagement scores had dropped by 12 percent. Employee turnover continues to increase and is driving up costs for the organization.

Goal: Hit over 85 percent in engagement to achieve targets and make the bonus. Increasing engagement will reduce company turnover and help increase cost efficiencies.

Gaps: Employees feel their managers are not committed to them or their development. They feel they are being expected to do more with less. This is requiring longer hours of work and less home-life balance. In addition, employees live in fear that their positions will be eliminated in the pursuit of cost efficiencies. Although there is plenty of opportunity for internal mobility, team members are being promoted prematurely, and they have little training to fully learn and master their roles, much less help their direct reports succeed in their roles. Culturally, the employees feel overworked and underappreciated. If they honestly address their feelings and concerns in company surveys, it can penalize their bonus.

Based on the goal and the gaps, if you were mentoring Sean, what kind of game plan would you help him establish?

There are no right or wrong answers here. Some coaches may advise him to tackle the engagement scores and get them up to keep the engine moving. This may not be the time to tackle a paradigm shift in the culture. Other coaches may suggest a more aggressive approach to solving the bigger underlying issues. There may also be a few coaches who would say this is a toxic culture and advise Sean to abandon ship to save himself. They may feel it is just a matter of time before the system goes after him personally.

The mentor agreement helps the process become laser-focused. Getting specific around a clear goal and identifying critical gaps makes creating a game plan simple and more impactful. This same process works whether dealing with complex corporate culture issues like Sean had or establishing ways to improve project-management skills. Clarity is crucial to creating change.

BEFORE THE AGREEMENT BEGINS

Before setting up any mentor agreement, there are some essential questions that need to be discussed between the mentor and mentee.

- What expectations do you both want to get from the relationship?
- What kind of format best supports these goals?
- How will you both deal with confidentiality?
- How does the mentee want to be pushed and challenged?
- What time frame will be established to work on this goal?
- What form of communication best fits both of you?
- Where and when will both parties meet? At work? Offsite?
- How direct and honest does the mentee really want the mentor to be?
- How will you both determine if the mentoring agreement was successful?
- What kind of accountability and follow-up is expected of both of you?

CHAPTER 12

Seven Traits of an Effective Mentor

A good mentor teaches you how to think, not what to think.

—ANONYMOUS

Years ago, I came across one study that found that over 50 percent of managers interviewed had people in their past who had helped them through mentoring relationships.[1] I would argue that those numbers are grossly understated. If we each think back to defining moments that have helped us achieve success personally and professionally, I believe we could identify important individuals who provided us with advice, direction, and opportunities along the way. These guides have helped shape the way we see and approach the world. They may have served as teachers or leaders,

---

1   *Coaching and Mentoring: How to Develop Top Talent and Achieve Stronger Performance* (Boston: Harvard Business School Press, 2004), 89.

but the mentoring role goes beyond simply providing new knowledge or skills. Mentorship is a unique relationship that inspires us and guides us to think differently about ourselves and the world around us. We often see many of the tactics used in the other coaching zones integrated in the mentorship process. However, the role of mentor is truly unique in helping leaders empower personal effectiveness in others.

Like the other zones in this book, mentoring is a coaching zone you're probably already engaged in formally or informally, so determine whether you're doing it effectively. Seven qualities contribute to making someone a great mentor.

COMPATIBILITY

The first quality is compatibility. Even if the mentor is an expert, unless the mentee and mentor get along, neither one will optimally benefit from the relationship, and the mentorship won't last long. For a mentorship to work, the mentee must be open to receiving the mentorship, and so mentor and mentee must be compatible.

INTEGRITY

Second, mentors must have integrity. A person who lacks integrity is like a house of cards: if you pull one of the bottom cards out, the whole thing collapses. Mentors must believe what they're saying. They're not just political or giving out textbook-correct answers. They're people who have been there and have genuine experience. For mentees to get the benefit of that experience, mentors must be honest and have the integrity to tell it like it really is.

EXPERTISE

The third trait, which has already been discussed briefly, is expertise specific to the area being mentored. Mentors need to not only know a lot about the subject but also have real-world experience and expertise in the area. In my work helping organizations establish mentorship programs, I've found people often choose mentors based on what's easy and convenient. They choose whoever is close by and won't take a lot of effort to build a relationship with. You get what you pay for, though, or you get back what you put in. Just because someone is nearby and okay at something doesn't mean they'll have enough expertise to guide you through dealing with your situation and improving. Mentorships are more effective when the mentor has expertise. Good leaders understand this and will guide and encourage their team members to seek out expertise instead of convenience.

Remember, if you have cancer, you're going to see an oncologist, not a general practitioner. And in fact, if you have leukemia, you're going to go one step further and find the best oncologist who specializes in that kind of cancer. If someone comes to you seeking mentoring, be honest with yourself about your expertise. Don't try to speak to everything. If you're not an expert in a certain area, or you continue to struggle with a particular issue, why would you want to be a mentor to someone having problems in that area?

AVAILABILITY

Fourth, mentors must be available. You could be the best mentor in the world, but if you don't have time to meet with or invest in someone, then those mentorships probably won't be good experiences.

MOTIVATION

The fifth trait is proper motivation. Mentors must have the right reason for entering a mentorship. Is it to help themselves or to help the mentee? Some people want to be mentors just to meet their personal goals or because it will help their career. The most successful mentors, though, mentor in the best interests of their mentees.

GROWTH

Sixth, great mentors continue to grow. They understand they haven't arrived yet and are open to further personal growth. As a result, they also understand mentees haven't arrived and are still growing too. It's much easier to work in partnership with someone when both parties are continuing to learn, grow, and develop.

VULNERABILITY

Finally, the seventh trait of great mentors is vulnerability. If someone has all the answers but no vulnerability, they'll be less likely to share, and a mentee won't be able to relate to them as well. We can relate to people who have made mistakes, gone through pain, and have been broken. It's harder to relate to someone who has never failed and who hasn't been through rough times or low moments in life. With people like that, we tend to think, "Oh, I'll never be able to live up to that." Great mentors are vulnerable and open about not only their successes but also their failures. They share their experiences of wins and losses because we can learn as much from the losses as the wins.

Of course, when you seek out a mentor who has vulnerabilities, you want to find someone who has learned to overcome them. For example, if you have problems with alcohol, you wouldn't go to an alcoholic who keeps struggling with alcoholism for help. You would go to someone who has overcome their alcoholism. Similarly, in the best mentorship relationships, the mentor should have overcome their major problems. The important thing is that they understand the pain the mentee is dealing with and are vulnerable enough to get in the mud with the mentee a bit. This way, the mentee doesn't feel like they're up against a superhero that naturally gets it. Rather, they're working with someone who understands there's a process to getting it and there will be struggles along the way.

As a leader, these are the traits you should focus on to be a good mentor. Before you take on a mentorship role with someone, make sure you have the compatibility, the integrity, the expertise, the availability, the proper motivation, the continual growth, and the vulnerability to be a good mentor.

GROUP MENTORING

While mentoring is often done one-on-one, it can happen in groups as well, primarily through mastermind groups.

Mastermind groups are groups of experts that discuss questions and ideas with you in a formal way, like in meetings. In a business, a mastermind group might look like a board of directors. They get together to share ideas and thoughts about what they're trying to accomplish, and as a group mentor/mentee, you can ask these people questions, and they can ask you questions too. They'll often dig in deeper and offer advice.

Groups like support communities allow peers and other participants to share ideas in a less formal setting. For example, Gregg Levoy, one of my favorite authors, does "popcorn-feedback" exercises in his workshops.

He'll ask someone, "What's something you're really passionate about and want to do?"

The person might say, "I want to start a dress shop."

"Okay, great. What are some things you can do right now to
get started?"

"I'm not sure," the person might say. "I'm really stuck and
don't know what to do."

Levoy will then bring in the audience and start a popcorn-
feedback session. Someone from the audience takes on the
role of scribe, writing down the ideas as everyone jumps in
to help this person brainstorm. People throw out all sorts
of ideas from their individual experiences. This is a wonderful tool that can move people from seeing something
from a small perspective to approaching their ideas, their
business, their dreams, or how they want to do their job, in
a whole new way.

GROUP MENTORING: PENNY'S PICKLE

As the manager of a government-assisted affordable apartments community, Penny dealt with a lot of high-risk and
high-intensity issues. For instance, in her environment,
she saw someone die at least once a month. Penny had to
deal with drug scandals and other issues many community

managers never deal with. She was in one of my leadership programs, and while we were talking about how to think outside the box, she said, "In my world, I can't do that." Penny talked about the issues she was facing and how overworked she was. She felt no one, including her, could handle it all, and I could hear in her voice how trapped she felt.

I could see other people in the class, her peers, and other folks from around the country, wanting to contribute their expertise, so I had the group do some popcorn feedback. Different ideas popped up, not just advice but ideas that stretched her idea of what she could do. The experience made Penny not only realize she had been thinking in a narrow way but it also opened her up to the idea of changing how she did her job. She went back and started mentoring her own people, enabling them to take on more and thus freeing her from some of the pressure that had been weighing on her.

Group mentoring has especially taken hold online as the internet is a wonderful tool to create mastermind groups and support group communities. For example, someone might post a question on LinkedIn asking how people would deal with something, and others respond, saying what they would do in that situation. There are all sorts of communities like this online that provide mentorship or feedback or help generate out-of-the-box thinking.

PART IV CONCLUSION

Mentorship can be a powerful tool and an effective coaching zone for you as a leader. This is your chance to share your expertise and experience. Wise mentors not only share their successes, but they also share the challenges they faced along the way. If you listen to seasoned leaders, the older they get, the more important leaving a legacy becomes. Younger leaders may spend more time focused on climbing the proverbial corporate ladder. At a certain point, leaders may find helping others in their career more fulfilling.

In Herman Melville's classic book, *Moby Dick*, there is a great line that says, "It is not down in any map; true places never are." I would say this describes the power of mentorship. People talk about the tools needed to be successful in management and leadership. I would argue that mentorship is a tool that is seldom discussed but one of the most rewarding and transformational, for the mentor and mentee.

I encourage you to review the seven traits of effective mentors and take a moment to evaluate yourself. What do you need to work on to be an effective mentor? If you do not already have a mentor, then who comes to mind that lives those traits that you would like to explore a mentor agreement with? If you are already a mentor to your team, how can you make these experiences more effective by using agreements and tools to focus your time and efforts?

WHAT IS MENTORING?

1. Mentoring is the process where two individuals enter into a learning relationship together that has focused objectives, established boundaries, and a clear timeline.

2. Mentoring is initiated when a team member/coachee essentially says, "I have a problem. Fix me."

3. In Zone 3, mentoring, the team member/coachee is aware of the coaching need.

4. Mentoring is an effective coaching tool when targeted, expert coaching that's specific to the team member/coachee's problem is needed. The leader/coach provides mentoring specific to the team member/coachee's individual needs, versus a spray of information typical of Zone 2, training.

5. The team member/coachee points out a problem and then seeks out a mentor to help them fix it through the mentoring process.

6. Mentoring provides the team member/coachee with an in-depth understanding of subject matter that cannot be satisfied through training.

7. In Zone 3, the leader/coach must be an expert in the subject they are coaching.

8. The leader/coach determines the mentoring topics.

9. The leader/coach also determines the action plan.

PART IV QUESTIONS FOR REFLECTION

1. What mentors have shaped your life and career today?
2. What behaviors did they demonstrate that had the greatest impact on you personally?
3. What do you need to change to become an effective mentor for others?

Part V

COLLABORATION

CHAPTER 13

Introduction to Zone 4: Collaboration

You cannot teach humans anything. You can only help them discover it within themselves.

—GALILEO

Zone 4, collaboration, is "I have a problem. Help me fix myself." This zone gets into the areas of executive performance and developmental coaching, in which the coach asks questions and lets people self-discover and figure out how to fix the problem themselves.

Collaboration is the process of recognizing the power within others and helping them create their own solutions by providing the right awareness, support, and environment to implement change.

This zone is ideal when the team member doesn't need someone else telling them what to do because they already have the answer inside. The coach's job is to create awareness for the coachee to explore the situation differently and then help them find a solution on their own. This zone helps them see things they haven't been able to see and gain a better understanding of what they already know.

Collaboration is very different than the other coaching zones. Every person involved in the collaborative relationship must want to be in that relationship. It happens because everyone involved chooses to be in the relationship together. You can't force someone into this zone.

Collaboration empowers the coachee to take back control of their lives. It's truly a process of empowerment, and that's one of the major differences between it and the other coaching zones. When you're giving feedback, it's your feedback. If you're mentoring someone, it's still your advice. Collaboration truly gives people an opportunity to control their own destinies—to make their own action plans and decide how they want to move forward.

THE COLLABORATIVE COACH: SARAH'S SECRET

Sarah, a director at a large telecommunications organization, had cultivated a unique relationship with her team that her peers did not enjoy with theirs. She managed a large group at work and was a single mom at home. Sarah was also the primary caregiver for her mother. With all her personal responsibilities, Sarah still managed to deliver 20 percent growth year after year in an organization where most people in her role saw losses those same years. What amazed the people about Sarah was not only her business results but that she still had time to have healthy relationships and fully engage with her family.

I wanted to find out what Sarah and her team knew that the rest of the leaders in the organization were missing. What was Sarah's secret? I set up a time to do a ride-along with her, visiting some of her stores.

At first, I asked Sarah questions about how much time she was working. The thought was that she was working longer and harder than others in her same role.

"What does a typical day look like for you?" I asked her.

"I get up and spend time with the kids before they go to school. Then I do some planning for the day to see where I need to focus, and I prioritize my time around new issues along with my usual work priorities."

"Do you start your day earlier than others?" I asked.

"Not really," she responded. "I work eight-to-five most days."

Sarah's peers were working sixty to eighty hours a week. I asked her, "Do you work later?"

"No, I have to go home and take care of my kids," she said. "I occasionally stay late, but not often."

Sarah's first stop that morning was at a store where the numbers were down. Before we went in, I asked her what she thought was going on there.

"I don't know," she told me. "That's what we're going to find out."

It wasn't until I walked into a store with Sarah and watched her interactions with her team that I really understood Sarah's secret. Leaders in her role usually tell everyone what's wrong and how to fix it. The first thing Sarah did was ask her people about themselves. "How are you? How are things going?" Her interactions with them were about who they were as people, not just what they were producing. The whole environment changed right away as she talked with them—with them, not at them.

After talking with everyone, Sarah pulled the store manager aside. Like a lot of leaders, she started asking him questions, but her questions were very different. Other leaders might cut to the chase, saying, "Here's what the numbers are. What are you doing to fix this? Why is this not done? When are you going to have this fixed?" Instead, Sarah asked the manager questions like, "What do you think is happening here? How are things going? What do you think the numbers are reflecting?" Then she let the manager talk about what was going on.

Sarah's approach sent the conversation in a totally different direction than I'd seen with other leaders at that company. Her questions enabled the managers to feel more comfortable and safe, able to honestly share what was affecting their business. Even when the manager began making excuses, Sarah knew how to steer the conversation away from factors beyond his control and refocus it on those factors he could control. Sarah accepted the fact that her managers were the experts and she was there to learn from them instead of acting like she was the expert, there to swoop in and tell them exactly what to do.

Sarah eventually asked the manager things like, "What do you want to do about this? How do you want to reshape this? What is that going to look like?" Through this series of questions, the manager eventually came up with his own direction of what he and his team were going to do and his own plans for how they were going to fix their store's problems.

This collaborative process allowed Sarah's team members to own the solution and feel empowered. As a result, they were more likely to be successful. Then, on subsequent return visits, Sarah praised her managers for their efforts. They got all the glory and the praise. After all, they had come up with their own solution, and it worked.

Sarah used collaboration to work with her teams to solve a problem. She ensured that her teams devised their own action plans. Sarah might make recommendations, but she always allowed her people to determine their own plan. She didn't always rely on collaboration, though. Sarah used all four zones to coach and manage her team, depending on the need. There were times when her team needed feedback, training, and mentoring.

In this example, her collaborative approach resulted in several benefits. For one, her team's results were far greater than others' results in the company. Her people were typically closer to the problems than she was and could often see things she couldn't. They were able to come up with innovative and creative solutions that Sarah and other people in the organization never would have dreamed about. In fact, her team's solutions often produced better results than her own solutions would have.

Her team's engagement scores were also far greater than other teams. Her team felt, regardless of what was happening in the company, their leader was invested in them and believed in who they were. Sarah's team also felt like a team, largely because they collaborated with each other, not just in-store but among different stores. Even though the stores were pegged against each other in some ways—like having to compete on the stack rankings—Sarah's market felt like a cohesive team working together for the good of the entire market and organization. The managers communicated with each other and acted like team members instead of competitors. Where did that behavior come from? It certainly wasn't financial. It was through collaboration.

Sarah also had fewer performance issues on her team. Instead of holding her team accountable all the time, she fostered a sense of responsibility and ownership among her team members. As a result, she didn't have to do a lot of corrective action because her people were self-motivated, self-guided, and held themselves accountable.

As a final benefit of collaboration, Sarah's team became so astute at working through issues and resolving them, they were in line to become potential leaders, capable of replacing Sarah and other people in her role throughout the company. Sarah had helped provide them with the leadership development they needed to address issues and get the best out of people. She had empowered them to become leaders themselves.

Sarah wasn't the hero, and a collaboration coach's goal should never be to be the hero. The coaching process she utilized and had in fact mastered, collaboration, allowed her people to become their own heroes.

Some people would chalk up Sarah's results to great stores, locations, or managers. She did have great stores and great managers, but they didn't start off that way. She'd cultivated that greatness. Sarah could take on problem stores and turn them around because it wasn't about starting off with a terrific location or great people. It was about developing what she had into something great. Sarah's story goes back to the principle that it's just as easy to do the right thing as it is to do the wrong thing. Sarah wasn't working any harder or any longer than other leaders at the company. She was simply doing different things that enabled her to get different results—better results.

To this day, years later and long after Sarah left the organization, people still talk about her and her impact on the people and the company. The relationships she developed with people went far beyond the typical relationship between a leader and a subordinate.

THE VESSEL AND THE ACORN

When I was first starting out in coaching, I was introduced to a book called *Coaching for Performance* by John Whitmore. In the book, the author uses an analogy about the difference between seeing our people as an acorn, versus viewing them as vessels.[1] Leaders who see their people as empty vessels focus on filling them up with knowledge and experience. In

1   Whitmore, *Coaching for Performance*, 9.

many cases, recruitment teams spend hours looking for the perfect candidate with a wealth of experience to fill a position. However, once those people are hired, leaders ignore the new recruits' experience, education, and expertise and let them know right away: "That's not how we do things around here. Just do what I tell you to do."

When a leader takes a vessel view of their team members, the focus remains on the leader, and everyone else is viewed as a minion whose job is to roll out the agenda and make the leader look good. These bright people with so much to offer must rely on the leader's detailed direction to complete a project.

Vessel-type leaders tend to be micromanagers. In many cases, they think they could do the job better than any of their people, and they fight the temptation to take on the project themselves. Worse, they sometimes go behind their people's backs to redo the work. Leaders who view their people as vessels tend to treat them like replaceable commodities. If one fails to meet the standards, it's easy to hire another recruit to pick up where they left off. Remember, in these situations, it is really about the leader, not the people.

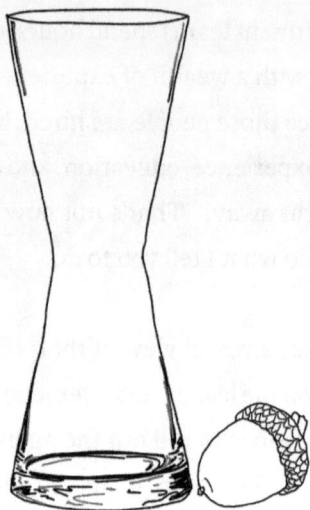

Leaders who see their people like acorns treat them radically different. Think of it this way: a tiny acorn can grow into an oak tree with an average height of over 150 feet. They can live to over two hundred years and grow to a circumference of six feet in diameter. No matter how creative or powerful a leader may be, they cannot make an oak tree. They can only grow a tree by creating the best environment possible: planting it in good soil, nurturing it, fertilizing it, and watering it. Ultimately, everything that tree needs is within that little acorn. It just needs the right environment to bring out its best. Leaders who view their people not as vessels but as acorns treat them as if they have unlimited potential. They create the right environments to nurture them and help them grow.

I recognize there are some situations where we need our people to follow certain rules and guidelines for a myriad of reasons, often due to legal implications. This doesn't discount the point of how to best approach them, though. People will live up to the expectations of the leader. If a leader treats people like vessels, then they will act like it. They will avoid creativity and innovation. They will wait for direction and only do what they are told with little regard to initiative. They will learn to expect very little credit for their work but accept the blame if something goes wrong. They will be fearful of losing their job and constantly wonder how they can get ahead within the organization with little opportunity to grow and develop.

On the other hand, leaders who see their people as acorns full of unlimited potential and who help nurture their abilities and skills create far better results. Their teams foster innovation and creativity. Their people take initiative, and when problems come up, each person owns their part of the setback and works to find a fresh solution. They have the freedom to fail, but more so, they have the freedom to succeed and showcase their abilities. They get credit for their work and learn the importance of working as a team. When you don't have to fight for praise, you find there is plenty to go around to everyone.

Remember Sarah? Sarah approached and led her people with a different mindset. She viewed them as people, not commodities—saw them as acorns, full of endless possibilities. Sarah learned how to collaborate with her people to bring out their best and allow them to grow into oak trees.

Take a moment to think about the vessel, the acorn, and your own coaching experiences.

- Which kind of leader would you like to be managed by?

....

- What environment would you thrive in?

....

- What kind of manager are you to your people currently?

....

- How do you need to shift in the way you think and treat your team members that would unlock their unlimited potential?

....

PERFORMANCE VS. DEVELOPMENTAL COLLABORATION

The two primary types of collaboration are performance collaboration and developmental collaboration.

Performance collaboration focuses on issues or goals the

coach wants to address with a team member. This could be metrics that need to be dealt with, a failure to do something, or a problem with a certain relationship—any sort of performance issue. The important distinction with performance collaboration is that you, as the leader, choose the topic that you and your team member address in the coaching session.

With developmental collaboration, the coachee chooses the topic. The leader asks, "Hey, what would you like to talk about?" and lets the other person talk about whatever is on their mind and how they want to personally develop.

The general rule between these two types of collaboration is, the more developmental collaboration coaching you do, the less performance collaboration coaching you will have to do. If you allow people to talk about their own needs and challenges, they are more likely to identify what's at the core of their problems than if you approach the coaching with your own agenda. Often, if you have a specific topic you want to discuss, it will come up in developmental coaching anyway.

Regardless of the type of collaboration, the goal of collaboration coaching is to help people see the bigger picture. Collaboration pulls that information out of the person by putting them in the right environment and asking the right questions. The person knows the correct answers and knows the right direction to go; they just need a little help to become aware of what they already know.

With both types of collaboration coaching—performance and developmental—there is always an action plan. If there is no action plan, you have not had a coaching session—just an enjoyable conversation.

There is always an action plan, and the coachee always determines the action plan. Always. Leaders often feel like they should determine the action plan because they know better, but that's not how collaborating works. If you're laying out the plan of action (such as discussing a performance improvement plan), you are providing feedback, not collaborating. It can be difficult to keep your thoughts to yourself because, as a leader, people are always coming to you for advice, but it's critical that you allow the collaboration coachee to determine their own plan.

Performance collaboration conversations can begin with statements such as:

1. I would like us to talk about...
2. I have something I would like your help with.
3. Based on the recent numbers (activities), I would like us to discuss...

Ask questions like these to get the developmental collaboration conversation started:

1. What would be important for us to discuss today?

2. Where would you like us to focus our time today?
3. What topic would help you the most?

You'll find more sample questions in the next chapter, "The RED Zone Collaboration Process," and in Chapter 17, "The Coach's Playbook."

DEVELOPMENTAL COACHING: CAMILA'S CATASTROPHE

Camila had been a leader and top performer in her organization for years, but recently, she was having problems. She was struggling operationally, failing to meet her numbers, and she wasn't being the leader she needed to be. Her manager explained Camila's situation and asked me to coach her but also noted, "Frankly, I think I'm going to have to terminate her, but I want to see if there's anything we can do to save her."

I asked her manager whether he wanted me to do performance collaboration with Camila, focusing on the three issues he had identified, or developmental collaboration, in which I would allow her to choose the topics for discussion. He didn't have a preference, so I chose developmental. I knew it would provide the results the manager wanted, and it would be a better experience for Camila.

Managers typically ask me to do performance coaching because they're focused on instant results and don't understand the value of developmental collaboration. If they instead introduced developmental coaching, which focuses more on the person, they could see long-term improvements and even better results.

While I didn't know Camila very well, I had a reputation around the company for being trustworthy, and I built on that trust by creating a safe environment for her to talk. It was important that her manager not be present, and we kept the fact that she was being coached between the three of us—Camila, her manager, and me—and HR. I did not want Camila to feel uncomfortable, embarrassed, or threatened by my presence, and so establishing and maintaining that confidentiality was critical to our coaching success.

I explained to her why we were meeting. "We're trying to help people develop and get better at what they're doing," I told her. "You're not in trouble, and there's no agenda here outside of the fact that I want to help you. We can work on whatever you want to." I then asked, "What would you like to talk about?"

Camila immediately identified her performance as something she wanted to talk about. She didn't mention operations or her role as a leader, so I didn't mention that either. For the time being, we focused on her performance.

At first, Camila blamed the company's products for her performance issues. I asked her, "What kind of products do you need?" Camila thought about the question and realized the products weren't the cause of her performance issues.

Next, Camila told me she needed better sales techniques. We talked about her current ones, and she evaluated each of them on a scale of one to ten. Camila gave herself nines and tens for almost every technique, so I said, "It sounds like these techniques are actually working for you. So what's really going on?"

As we continued through the collaborative process, Camila began to cry. She said, "I moved in with my boyfriend a few months ago. He's a great salesperson, and he's been making fun of me and my sales ability. To pay my part of the rent, I have to hit 150 percent of my metrics."

Camila recognized that her situation at home was affecting her performance, and I asked her what she wanted to do next to help her situation.

"I need to go home and have a conversation with my boy-friend," she said. "And I need to relax a little when I'm with my customers. I need to do what I can do—be the best me I can be—and then let the numbers fall where they fall."

Without any advice from me, Camila had put together her own action plan.

When you provide an environment of safety and trust, focus on the person instead of the issues, and ask the right questions, people will quickly identify their challenges. They know they have them—it's not a secret to their management or to them, but only they know the true cause. Camila knew what was going on. She just needed the right kind of coaching to allow her to talk about it and permission to come up with her own solution.

People will come up with their own solution to their performance problems if you allow them to, and developmental coaching allows them to do that. Once the coachee realizes you are there to support them—and not tell them what they did wrong or tell them what to do about it—the atmosphere around the coaching changes. The coachee can then view coaching as a positive experience because you are showing that you care about their thoughts and ideas, and that you care about them as an employee and as a person. It is like a vote of confidence from management instead of a stain on their record.

This shift in atttude toward coaching leads to a better experience for the coach, the coachee, and the company. Ultimately, it is the process of collaborative coaching that allows the coachee to be their own hero.

When I followed up with Camila a month later, her numbers were at 150 percent, and she was much happier and more relaxed. Her manager told me, "She's leading the team, her operations are perfect, and her sales are up. She's doing an exceptional job. It's like I have her all over again, brand new."

As leaders, we want to make things about what we see as the problem, like operations issues or performance metrics, but team members know what the real issues are. Our job is to let them talk it out so they can realize what they need to fix, and then allow them to form an action plan. I could have had Camila talk about the things I wanted to talk about, but she had much more information than I did. She was living the problem. Camila didn't have a sales issue, she had a personal issue, and she was able identify it and fix her situation. She worked on it, and her numbers went back up to where they needed to be. And even though we didn't talk about operations or leadership at all, she fixed those problems too. That is the value of developmental collaboration.

RESISTANCE TO COLLABORATION

A coachee's resistance to coaching is typically caused by a resistant coach. The biggest failures in collaboration are often due to the skill and attitude of the coach, not the person being coached. Remember you, as the coach, are the limitation of what your people will or will not do.

When I work with leaders on the process of collaboration, I often meet resistance. People might say, "This is great and all, but you don't know my team." They say collaboration won't work for them because they've inherited angry people, or they have this one person who isn't coachable. "Collaboration just doesn't work," they say. When I meet resistance like this, it usually isn't the attitude of the coachee that I must help reshape but the attitude of the leader. Oftentimes, the coachee is simply acting as a reflection of the leader. If I can help the leader shift their mindset, the coachee's mindset typically shifts as well.

THE RESISTANT COACH: WANDA'S WHALE

Wanda was part of a leader's group that was learning better coaching skills. She said one of her people was impossible to coach. Wanda had made up her mind that this person wasn't coachable.

"This is my Moby Dick," she told me. "I cannot win this."

Rather than offer to coach the person for her, I asked Wanda if, as a group, we could step through the collaboration process for this situation so she could learn how it works. Wanda agreed and started sharing what she thought were the key facts of the situation. "Let me tell you," she said, "I have done everything I can to help this person."

There was nugget number one: she had done "everything" she could to help this person. Wanda was telling herself a story about the situation instead of calling out the facts. Next, she pointed out that even though she had tried everything, nothing worked or would ever work.

"Okay," I said. "Are we having a conversation about how you're going to terminate this employee, or is there still a possibility for you to believe in her and rehabilitate her? If you believe there's no hope, is it fair to expect her to see any hope in her situation?"

Wanda realized she needed to change something in herself and how she saw her employee. She was approaching the situation as if she wanted the person to change.

This leader had started the conversation trying to prove her team member wasn't coachable, but the real uncoachable person in the room was her. Once Wanda started to shift her mindset and become coachable, she began to believe her team member was coachable too.

Techniques exist to help resistant people come around in coaching, but resistance often comes from the coach, not the coachee. If you hit resistance in a coaching session, first ask yourself what work you have to do. Ask yourself, "What do I really believe about this person? What story have I told myself about this situation? What am I trying to accomplish with this coaching? Am I trying to help this person develop, or am I working on an exit strategy? Is there trust and safety in this environment?"

CHAPTER 14

The RED Zone Collaboration Process

Today I will do what others won't, so tomorrow I can accomplish what others can't.

—JERRY RICE

In football, you're able to score statistically higher when you get into the red zone, the area between the twenty-yard line and the goal line—that's where you have a better chance of making a field goal or touchdown. It's not just about the physical proximity but the mental proximity. When you're in the red zone, you get excited, thinking, "I'm in the scoring zone. I can do it." Your mental acuity jumps up, heightening your awareness.

In many ways, collaboration done well is the RED Zone of coaching.

THE **RED ZONE** PROCESS

REFLECT

Build awareness of the problem to be worked on. This stage takes up 75% of the process, and comes in 3 steps.

1. REVIEW RESULTS
Look at metrics, performance indicators, facts and stories to determine the focus of the coaching session.

2. GUIDE THE GOAL
Develop a SMART goal to define what you will achieve.

3. RATE THE REALITY
Assess the effectiveness of the current plan.

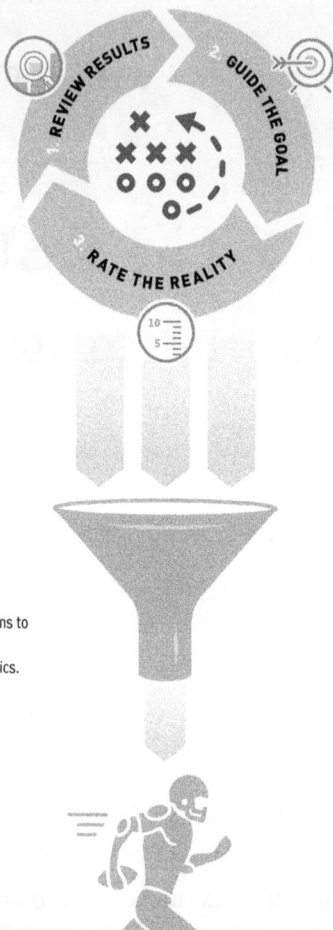

EXPLORE

Brainstorm innovative ideas and plans to achieve the goal. Begin with broad questions and funnel down to specifics.

DECIDE

Establish the action plan, timeline, and specific times to follow up.

In situations where collaboration coaching fits, if you get people into the RED Zone, the opportunities for achieving your goals and getting greater results skyrocket over those possible with feedback, training, or mentoring. RED Zone collaboration intensifies everything you're trying to do in the coaching process. You're more engaged mentally and can achieve better, more long-term results.

RED Zone collaboration is an effective framework for guiding leaders through this process. Three stages comprise this process and make up the acronym RED—Reflect, Explore, and Decide.

REFLECT

The first stage of the RED Zone, reflect, uses the triage wheel to help you assess, "What is going on? Where's the pain point?" This stage in the process helps the coach and the coachee understand the real issue. It doesn't matter how good your coaching process is—if you're dealing with the wrong topic, you'll always end up with the wrong solution.

REFLECT

Build awareness of the problem to be worked on. This stage takes up 75% of the process, and comes in 3 steps.

1. REVIEW RESULTS
Look at metrics, performance indicators, facts and stories to determine the focus of the coaching session.

2. GUIDE THE GOAL
Develop a SMART goal to define what you will achieve.

3. RATE THE REALITY
Assess the effectiveness of the current plan.

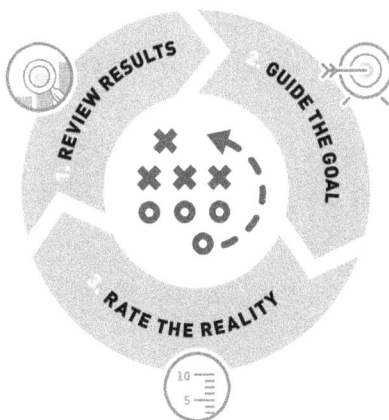

Remember when Camila told me her problems at work were due to the product? Upon reflection, she realized the issue wasn't the product but a problem she was dealing with at home. Getting down to the real problem is the core of the reflect stage, and so it takes the longest. In fact, about 75 percent of RED Zone collaboration coaching time should be spent in the reflect stage, with the explore and decide stages making up the remaining 25 percent.

That time distribution often scares people. They don't want to reflect; they want to talk about how to fix the problem and get results. Resist the urge to skip this stage, because if you don't allow the coachee enough time to reflect, you won't get the results you want. Leaders typically want to brainstorm options right away because fixing problems and getting results is what they do every day. "You have an issue with your numbers. What do you want to do to fix it?" or "Here's what I want you to do to fix it." The problem with skipping straight to a solution is, you skip the very important step of creating awareness for the coachee.

Three steps comprise the reflect phase: review the results, guide the goal, and rate the reality.

REVIEW THE RESULTS

If it's your first coaching session with a team member, review what you want to talk about, asking questions like, "What's our purpose in getting together? Are there metrics that are not being met? Are there behaviors holding you back from exceptional results? What is really taking place here?"

If you've had previous coaching sessions with this person, start with a review of the last session.

If you're taking a developmental approach, let the coachee take charge of the goal. To review the results, you might ask, "How did our last session go for you?" or "What are you working on now? How is that going?" Give the coachee a chance to assess and determine what's important to them and what they want to talk about. This is also where you start to discuss the pain points the coachee is feeling and wants to address.

The Stories We Tell Ourselves

Reviewing the results is also about fact-finding. As human beings, we tend to tell ourselves stories. Then, we tend to fit the facts to justify the stories we tell ourselves. For example, recently I was trying to get in touch with a friend. After several attempts to reach this person via phone and text, I became frustrated. I wondered if I had done something to offend them. I began to think they were just being rude and unprofessional. These were the stories I told myself. The more days that passed without a response from them, the more my stories felt justified. Eventually, I received a call.

The friend had been in the hospital for over a week. They had had a severe heart attack and were fighting for their life. I allowed the stories I told myself to affect my emotions and thoughts about this friend but had been completely wrong about what the reality was.

A key role of the coach is helping the coachee review the facts or acknowledge the lack of facts. This is a critical step in creating a climate of change. Until we face the reality of our stories, we can't move on to create new ways of thinking. Just as I had blinded myself to the facts with the story I told myself about my friend, the person you're coaching may be blinded by their own story.

Verbal Clues to Storytelling

You can sometimes identify when a person is telling themselves stories by listening for verbal clues. One of the most common verbal clues is the use of superlatives or absolutes. For example, when the coachee is explaining the cause of a problem or why a solution doesn't work, they might say, "I have the worst region," or "My manager always picks on me." They may also exaggerate: "I've tried doing it that way a million times."

To move past the stories, provide the facts, then let them tell their side of the story based on the facts. Make the facts the story. Do they really have the worst region? When has their manager actually picked on them? How many times have they tried a particular solution?

As a coach, be aware of your own use of superlatives and absolutes. If you tell someone, "You're always late," they can argue with that statement because they're not late every single day. But if you tell them, "You have been more than twenty minutes late seven separate times in the past month," they can't dispute that. It's a fact. In coaching situations, people accept criticism better and resist less when you start with the facts. If you don't start with the facts—the reality— you coach to a story.

GUIDE THE GOAL

Reviewing the results—reviewing the metrics, performance indicators, facts, and stories, and determining what they tell you—leads you to what is important, and then you can guide the goal.

When you're collaborating, there may be times when you work on a couple of things at a time, but for the most part, you should focus on one goal per coaching session. Often- times, you don't have time to do more than that. If a coachee comes up with more goals than you can cover, as the coach, it's your responsibility to help them prioritize their problems and goals, and then decide what they need to work on first. This may sound something like, "It sounds like you have several items you want to cover; however, in the twenty minutes we have today, which goal is most important to you?" That helps them prioritize the goals and keeps the conversation targeted. It also helps reduce the chances of overwhelming them with too many issues and goals in one session. Addressing too many goals at once is ineffective, and expecting a good result is unrealistic.

As the leader and coach, you can help your coachee further define their goals by teaching them about SMART goals and asking them questions that help them define their own SMART goals.

SMART Goals

SMART is an acronym that leaders use to simplify their goals. The definitions vary, but the point of SMART in coaching is to help the leader and team member focus their time and efforts on goals that are specific, measurable, agreed to, realistic, and time-based.

SMART GOALS

SMART goals are specific, measurable, agreed to, realistic, and time-based. Compare the following statements:

Specific:

- "I will be more valuable to my team" is not specific.
- "I will be more valuable to my team by increasing my sales" is specific.

Measurable:

- "I will increase my sales a lot" is not measurable.
- "I will increase my sales by ten percent" is measurable.

Agreed to:

- "You will increase your sales by ten percent" is not agreed to.
- "I will increase my sales by ten percent" is agreed to.

Realistic:

- "I will increase my sales by ten percent tomorrow" is not realistic.
- "I will increase my sales by ten percent within one quarter" is realistic.

Time-Based:

- "I will increase my sales by ten percent eventually" is not time-based.
- "I will increase my sales by ten percent this quarter" is time-based.

Now, compare these two statements:

- "You will be more valuable to your team and increase your sales a lot tomorrow or eventually."
- "I will be more valuable to my team by increasing my sales by ten percent this quarter."

Which goal is more likely to be achieved?

Specific

Many goals die before they begin. Goals need to be specific
and focused for the coachee to understand exactly what
it is they're shooting for or expected to achieve. If a team
member says, "I need to work harder," what does this mean?
How will they ever know if they achieve the goal? Look at
the difference between that statement and saying, "I need
to improve my performance in customer retention scores
by 20 percent by the end of the month." Which goal is more
likely to achieve the results? Specific goals provide clarity
and focus.

Measurable

At the end of the allotted time, an individual must be able to
show they either hit their goal or didn't. SMART goals are
tied to measurable indicators, not just feelings of success.
What does it mean if I say, "I want to get healthy in my life?"
How will I know if I'm healthy? If I say, "I need to exercise
three days a week for thirty minutes a day," I can track the
goal. This clarity helps me not only to achieve the goal but
also to hold myself accountable for reaching it.

Agreed To

If a coachee is assigned a goal and they have no input, it
usually leads nowhere. Whether they self-sabotage or just
ignore it altogether, a goal mandated without buy-in pro-

duces inferior results. This does not mean a coachee always gets to pick the goals they pursue. It does mean they're more likely to achieve a goal if they agree to take it on.

Feeling in control of our lives is paramount to growth and achievement. Buy-in helps us continue when the goal becomes challenging and difficult. When the desire to give up and give in hits, that personal commitment often sustains our willpower and helps us stay the course even as obstacles surface. It helps us work harder and longer. It provides us with a reason to sacrifice for success.

Realistic

Goals can be specific and measurable, but if they are not realistic, they will ultimately fail. In the sales world, when sales makers get behind on their quotas or key performance indicators (KPIs), they might attempt a Hail Mary last-minute drive to finish the month or the quarter. They throw logic out the window and make a mad dash for the finish line. Sometimes these last-minute drives produce a unicorn finish, but those are rare and often not the best use of our time. We increase our odds of success by pushing ourselves toward goals that challenge us but are within the realm of what we can accomplish, given our skills, the time frame, and the circumstances.

Time-Based

Goals require a deadline. A finish line creates urgency and allows the person to manage their time to the goal. If we just say we want to make a sale at some point, our ability to put a plan in place that gets us to the finish line is limited. The more specific the time, the more likely we are to achieve the goal.

For example, saying, "I want to finish the report sometime next week," is not the same as saying, "I will finish the report by Friday at five p.m." Do you feel the difference between the two statements? That "five p.m." adds a level of urgency that the vague timeline doesn't. It also provides a clear window for someone to expect the completion of the report. If it doesn't happen, the time-based element makes accountability easy and specific.

Too often, people choose vague, broad goals that aren't SMART, with no clear steps to take to achieve those goals. If someone tells me, "I want to improve my leadership abilities," I guide that goal into something SMARTer. I might start by asking, "What are some specific areas you want to work on in your leadership?" They'll give me something a bit more specific, and then we keep funneling the goal, stripping away ambiguity, by asking questions that lead to a definition that is specific, measurable, agreed to, realistic, and time-based.

The coachee must be able to state their goal as a single sentence, SMART goal before they move to the next step. Once the SMART goal is set, the process moves much faster. For example, "By the end of today's coaching session, I want to have a solid plan for increasing my performance by ten percent by the end of the month." That's a SMART goal!

RATE THE REALITY

After the coachee sets a goal, the next step in the reflect stage is to rate the reality. In this step, the coach and coachee collaborate to evaluate what the team member is currently doing to address the issue and work toward the goal.

Many leaders don't recognize the importance of this step, but people will not move to a new plan until they're convinced their old plan doesn't work. This is so important that it bears repeating: the coachee will not move to a new plan until they accept the fact that their current plan is not working.

The coach may push to explore new options, but whether subconsciously or consciously, the coachee will continue to push their current solution until they acknowledge it doesn't produce the results they want and need.

REPEATING STORIES: WHEN A
COACHEE DOESN'T FEEL HEARD

- A key skill in all coaching zones is the ability to listen and hear the team member/coachee. A leader coach may think they're hearing a coachee when they're not, or they may be hearing them, but the coachee doesn't feel like they're being heard. When this happens, the coachee may repeat the same message repeatedly.

- Listen for key transition points to help you understand where people are. If the coachee keeps repeating the same story over and over, that may signify they feel they're not being heard or that the coach hasn't acknowledged their opinion, complaint, or message.

- In the reflect phase, you will often hear repeating stories. You need to acknowledge those stories and help people move on. If they can't get past their old stories—which is what the reflect stage is designed to help them do—they won't be able to explore a new way of understanding their problems.

In Chapter 17, "The Coach's Playbook," you'll learn how to manage this issue and talk to a coachee who feels they're not being heard.

To help them get past this phase, ask the coachee to list their current solutions—all those things they are doing to solve their problem. Then have the coachee rate those solutions in terms of their effectiveness in achieving the goal. You can ask, "On a scale of one to ten, ten being the highest, how is that working for you?" After they score everything, reveal to them that anything below an eight isn't working and then ask them what that says about their current strategies. "So what does this tell us about your plan?"

Before you can move on, you need to hear them say, "It's not working."

Now, they won't always need to scrap everything from their old plan. There may be some parts that are effective and worth salvaging. But you must hear some variant of those key words, "It's not working," before moving on. You must get the coachee to acknowledge at least part of their old plan doesn't work, or they won't be able to move on to fresh solutions.

One popular solution that people cling to, which isn't effective at all, is what I call the "nothing phenomenon." For example, let's say someone wants to get into mountain climbing and tells me, "I want to go climb fourteeners, David." By the way, "fourteeners" are 14,000-foot peaks, and hiking to their summits is a popular hobby in some areas of the country, like Colorado.

I'll say, "Great. What are you currently doing to achieve that goal?"

And the person will say, "Nothing."

"On a scale of one to ten, how is that plan working?" I'll ask.

When I ask someone to rate "nothing" on a scale of one to ten, the usual answer is five. How can doing nothing rate a five? It does not produce anything, but for some reason, many people think doing nothing eventually accomplishes something. They believe they don't have to change their plan but can keep doing nothing to achieve their goal.

People will continue with a current plan if they feel it produces results, so you must help them come to grips with the fact that doing nothing does not produce results. You can say, "You scored nothing as a five. That means fifty percent of the time doing absolutely nothing is helping you work toward your goal. Is that correct?"

At that point, they will probably say, "Well, not really."

"Okay, then what do you really rate nothing?"

"Zero."

Rating the reality is a way to break someone out of the cycle of thinking they can keep doing nothing or keep using their old strategies and behaviors. At this point, people are forced to change. That happens when they say, "My plan isn't working. I need to do something different."

What if you ask your coachee to rate their current solutions and they rate them as nines and tens? In that case, ask, "Is this really a problem?" or "Okay, then are we talking about the right thing?" Maybe the coachee has chosen a goal they've already achieved because they don't want to talk about the real issues. If their current plan is working, go back to the initial steps of the reflect phase to identify the real problem and determine the right goal.

EXPLORE

Once the coachee has accepted their old plan isn't working and they need a new plan, move on to the explore phase, where you explore innovative ideas and plans to achieve the goal.

EXPLORE

Brainstorm innovative ideas and plans to achieve the goal. Begin with broad questions and funnel down to specifics.

Have you ever ridden in a car with a driver who wanted to get to the destination as fast as possible with no concern for the comfort level of the passengers? The driver may arrive at the destination quickly, but with a car full of sick people who didn't enjoy the ride or get much out of the experience. That's what happens in direct-line thinking. It's not a pleasant experience for passengers, and it's not an effective method for leading collaboration coaching. Effective leaders/coaches must learn to think less about the speed of arriving at a solution and think more about the impact of the process on the team member/coachee.

In collaboration, there is a natural tendency to ask closed-ended questions and inspire closed-ended thinking to hurry a solution, but the direct way isn't the best way or even the fastest. Instead of taking a direct-line approach, starting wide—with open-ended questions—allows you to narrow things down to a more accurate solution. This approach is often faster, too, because you won't have to keep revisiting the same topic over and over.

To get people moving toward a new way of thinking, imagine a funnel. At the top of the funnel, ask broad questions. Then, as you get answers, ask more questions to get more specific answers. This is like the method used in the reflect stage—start broad and then narrow things down. To open the dialogue for a new plan, simply start over at the top of the funnel.

I recommend asking magic wand or lottery questions: "If you had a magic wand you could wave to make anything happen, what would you do?" or "If you won the lottery and had the money to do whatever you wanted, what would you do?" I like these kinds of questions because people often will not explore new ideas if they feel their situation is hopeless or if there's always going to be obstacles. As the coach, part of your job is to remove the obstacles, and these magic wand and lottery questions do that. They get people thinking in terms of what they would do if there were no barriers. People need to think about the solution for a while without worrying about not having the ability, budget, or resources to do it.

Many leaders get nervous with this type of question because they think people will simply say, "I'd wave my wand and make the problem go away." That may happen, but people won't usually go to absurd extremes with their responses. Remember, they want to solve this problem as much as or more than you do. If they do answer that way, acknowledge it and ask, "Great. What else would you do?"

You can also say, "Tell me more about that." Or, "What would that look like?" In this way, you move down that funnel and narrow the broad idea into a solution that's more specific and defined.

BRAINSTORMING IS A JUDGE-FREE ZONE

When you're brainstorming, anything goes. If someone says, "If I had a magic wand, I'd have us go to the moon and start projects there," don't bat an eye. Just write it down. The team member may be testing you to see whether they really can propose any idea. If you respond, "Well, that's absurd," you're proving to them only certain ideas are okay. It's important that you do not discount any ideas even if they're absurd, unreasonable, or not feasible because this is your team member's brainstorming session, not yours. When you open the brainstorming up to literally any idea, including the extreme ones, you give them the freedom to really think outside the box. Write down every idea and then ask, "What else?"

It's important to remain neutral and refrain from judging any of the ideas, either positively or negatively. If you say, "Well, that's dumb," or "Oh, that's a really clever idea," you influence their brainstorming process. If you show favoritism toward one way of thinking, they may feel they have to go in that direction. If you indicate you don't like a certain idea, they will avoid further ideas in that direction and may shut down in general, thinking they can't open up to you without being ridiculed. As their leader, stay completely neutral in this process.

Some people, especially if there's a trust barrier, will answer, "I don't know. What do you think I should do?"

This is an important trap to watch out for as a coach. If someone says this, you may think, "Well, now they're giving me permission to give them the answer." What that person is really doing is trying to avoid doing their own work, but as Jim Rohn once said, "You can't hire someone else to do your push-ups for you."

Don't get sucked into giving them the answer just because they asked. If you were in one of the other zones—feedback, training, or mentorship—it would be fine to provide the answer, but in this case, that's not your role. You're not to give them the answer, even though you may want to and think you have a great solution. The point of collaboration is for the coachee to work through the problem to get to their own solution.

If a team member/coachee tries to pass the buck by saying, "I don't know. What do you think I should do?" instead of caving and giving them the answer, say, "You know what? I think you really do know, and I believe you have some great thoughts and ideas about this. So if you could do anything, what are some things you would do?" This way, you put the brainstorming process back on them and guide them to that place of solutions instead of giving them a solution. Some people are afraid to open up in the collaboration process because they don't want to change. They will try to push things off on you, and you must continue to put the responsibility of thinking and solving back on them.

Everyone is different, and you must allow your coachee

to brainstorm, until they are done. I have found the best ideas tend to happen after the first two or three things suggested. In the brainstorming process, your job is to help dig out all the information. If someone says something broad, pull out specific information by saying, "Tell me more about that." Keep asking questions until they have nothing else to say. Be careful not to close people off by assuming they're done.

For example, it's important to say, "What else?" instead of "Anything else?" because the question "What else?" assumes there's more to be shared. It's like saying, "There's more in you. Keep it coming." On the other hand, "Anything else?" indicates you want the coachee to finish up. It's like saying, "Is there anything else? I'm trying to wrap this up." Asking "Is there anything else?" is a closed-ended question, too, allowing them to end the conversation with a simple yes or no. Don't let them off the hook that easy. There is almost always more to say.

Sometimes people give you lots of information, and sometimes they only give you a little. Let them dictate when the brainstorming is done. When you ask, "What else?" and they say, "There's nothing else" or "I'm done" or something similar, then the brainstorming is finished.

Leaders and team members sometimes rely on hope strategies instead of valid options in the explore stage.

A young salesperson once told me, "You know my problem? I just need to work harder." That was his whole plan.

"Okay," I said. "At the end of the month, how will you know you have worked harder?"

"Well, I just will. I'll just know it."

That's not a SMART goal, and it's not an acceptable option to settle on in the explore stage. People sometimes pick goals and strategies that aren't SMART to avoid being held accountable by their leaders or by themselves. Sometimes leaders also let people off the hook by giving them impossible, unattainable goals because they need a quick solution—even when they know it won't work.

As a coach, it's your job to make sure people's goals and strategies are SMART so they'll be set up for success. Dig deeper and ask, "Okay, what do you want to work harder at?"

"At talking to more customers," they might reply.

"Okay, what would you say to those people?"

"Well, I want to talk more about these specific things about our product and services."

"Okay. How many people are you currently talking to, and how many more do you want to talk to each month?"

"I talk to eighty people a month now and would like to talk to twenty more."

"All right, so you feel like success would be talking to twenty more people about these specific products and services by the end of this month?"

"Yes."

Now the team member has a plan that is tangible and realistic. They have a SMART goal and a much higher chance of achieving the desired results.

FREEDOM TO FAIL

Part of brainstorming and exploring is realizing no matter what the coachee decides, you must let them fail. Let people try things and make mistakes. If I'm coaching someone who is struggling in a certain area, I may know from my personal experience that the plan they've come up with isn't going to work. My role in collaboration is not to speak up and say, "You know, I've tried that, and it doesn't work. You need to think of something else." It's not my job to judge those things or get too involved, especially when brainstorming and exploring options.

Let's say someone is pursuing a goal they've never pursued before, a personal goal. Maybe they say, "I want to go back to college," and then you ask, "What do you need to do to start that process?" They may not have any idea what the steps are to go back to college. At that point, it's easy for you to want to jump in as the expert, saying, "Well, when I went to college, here's what I did. Here's who you need to talk to, and here's what you need to do." That's mentoring—giving answers. In the collaboration process, you shouldn't be the expert. It's much more important to let the people you're coaching find their own solutions.

If the coachee doesn't have the answers, you can still walk them through this process without giving them answers. Ask, "Who do you need to talk to this week to get started on going back to school?" or "Where can you research to find out what you need to know to do this?"

If they don't know where to start, help them put together a plan to find the information. Perhaps they have a goal of improving their time management skills. Instead of acting as the expert in time management and mentoring them, turn them loose to discover the information on their own. Ask, "Where can you go to explore more about time management?"

"Well, maybe I can look it up on Google."

"Yes, where else?"

"I can go to the library."

In this explore phase, be flexible and stay out of their way so they explore solutions on their own.

TRUST THE PROCESS

Leaders wonder, "When can I give them some options?" When you're learning how to be a collaborative coach, I recommend avoiding giving options.

We're all advice junkies. We get excited by the thought of giving people ideas, and it's too easy to get carried away, and just because it's our idea doesn't mean it's the best idea for that coachee with that problem in that situation. We're also not allowing the growth that's possible in collaboration coaching. When we give advice, we're not collaborating—we're mentoring.

Once you become more experienced—once you trust the process and learn people finding their own solutions is better than you giving them the solutions—you can start to give suggestions but ask permission first. "Do you mind if I offer a single suggestion?" Sometimes the coachee may say no, and that's okay. You must respect that and not be offended by it. In most cases, especially when you're the coachee's manager, they won't say no. In those instances, give the caveat, "Feel no obligation to do this." The people you coach often feel they must take your suggestion because you're their leader, so giving them this caveat frees them to pursue their plan, not yours.

Even when you get to a point where you occasionally give suggestions, I caution you to do so sparingly. Advice in collaboration is like cayenne pepper. It can add a powerful flavor to the coaching process, but if you use too much, it can spoil the whole meal. The coachee may begin to feel you're steering them in a certain direction, and suddenly it's no longer about them and their ideas but about you and your ideas.

People want others to do their work for them. If you give too much advice, the coachee will let you take over. Why in the world would they do the work if you're willing to do it for them? If the coachee doesn't do the work, you may cheat them out of the development process. When you rob them of the experience of finding their own answers, you also rob them of the resulting impact from the search and experience. The goal of collaboration isn't to get results as fast as possible but to get the best results possible.

The explore phase is over when the coachee says, "I'm done. I have no more ideas." Now you have some clear options to choose from.

DECIDE

Once the coachee is done exploring ideas, repeat all the options with verification and paraphrasing. Then transition to the decide phase.

Verification and paraphrasing are used to ensure that you and the person you're coaching agree on what's been said. Verification is specific and exact, while paraphrasing is a general summary of the conversation. An example of verification is, "You said you want a cold sandwich with mayonnaise, mustard, lettuce, cheese, pickles, and onions, or a hot sandwich with just cheese, right?" Paraphrasing the conversation would be, "You said you want a cold sandwich with everything on it, or a hot sandwich with cheese, right?"

Then, in the decide phase, you might say something like, "It sounds like you've narrowed your lunch choices to a cold sandwich with everything or a hot sandwich with cheese. Which of these would you like to move forward with?" In the case of an actual coaching scenario where you're discussing something more important than lunch, you might instead say, "It sounds like you have plans A, B, C, and D in mind. Which one would you like to move forward with?"

DECIDE

Establish the action plan, timeline, and specific times to follow up.

Then let them choose what they want to do. They may say, "I want to do all of them." They may not reasonably have the time to do all of them, so your job as coach is to bring them back to SMART again by asking, "Do you have the time to do all these things with the limitations and scheduling obstacles you have?" At that point, they'll likely say no, and then you can ask, "If you had to choose only three of these items, which would you choose?" Part of your job as coach is to help them see how they can simplify by narrowing their options. Another way to convey this idea is by saying, "You can always come back to more options next month, but for this month, which of these things are priorities for you?" In this way, you can guide them toward creating SMART targets.

Once the coachee chooses a goal, there are two actions you should take to set them up for success with their action plan. First, establish when the team member is going to move forward on their choices, and second, establish when you are going to follow up with them.

ESTABLISH A TIMELINE

They need a timeline, so "When are you going to do that by?" is a critical question for you to ask. You want the timeline to be specific.

Let's say your coachee says, "I'm going to have a conversation with a recruitment counselor."

You should then ask, "When are you going to do that?"

"By next week."

"When next week?"

"Friday."

"Friday by when?"

"Friday by five o'clock."

"Okay, great. So by Friday at five p.m., you will have had a conversation with a recruitment counselor. Is that right?"

"Yes."

With a clear timeline, this plan is now a locked-in goal. The goal has become very real, and the team member has committed to it. They can't put it off until later. When five o'clock rolls around on Friday, they will know whether they've achieved their goal.

Sometimes a team member will respond to your initial timeline question with something like, "Well, I don't know when my boss will be available to talk."

"Okay. With that in mind, when do you think you'll have that done by?"

"I think by five o'clock on Tuesday."

"Does that give you plenty of room in case your boss isn't available to talk about it?"

"Yes."

"Okay, great."

Help your team member create dates and times for every single action they're willing to move forward with.

FOLLOW UP

After establishing a timeline, determine when you will follow up with the coachee. In some cases, collaboration sessions are an in-and-out, one-time-only relationship where there isn't a follow-up, but if you are a leader collaborating with one of your team members, a follow-up is critical to maintaining that ongoing relationship and investment you have in them. One of the biggest hurdles with coaching team members is the lack of a follow-up.

Like setting the timeline for the action plan, set a specific time to follow up. If you're doing developmental coaching, ask the coachee when they want to follow up. If you're doing performance coaching, you can set the follow-up time. "Let's follow up with that next Tuesday," or "Let's follow up with that next month in our one-on-one." If something is urgent—perhaps the team member is really struggling and is at a critical point—you may not be able to wait a month or even a week. In those cases, you may want to follow up the next day, in the next few days, or even in a couple of hours. Set the follow-up according to the needs of the situation. An urgent situation requires urgent follow-up, but if the situation isn't urgent, you could follow up in a month or two months.

At this point in the decide phase, leaders like to ask, "What do you need from me or others to help support you in this?" Be careful when offering support in this way. It is easy to slip into collective language like, "What are *we* going to do?" Collaboration coaching is not about "we;" it's about the team member. Because collaboration is focused on the coachee, not on us collectively, do not use the universal "we." Make sure you're saying, "What would *you* like to follow up with? What would *you* like to do?" This doesn't mean you don't offer support. You can offer your services; you just can't own those services. Ask, "What support or resources do you need so you can be more effective in achieving this?"

CELEBRATING ALONG THE WAY

It's also critical to have celebration points and milestones. You can incorporate these celebrations into your follow-ups. In many cases, leaders are so fixated on problems that they forget to celebrate the wins. Wins build more wins, so as the coach, part of your job is acknowledging and celebrating momentum and little steps along the way. People sometimes get so focused on big goals that they don't stop to celebrate the achievement of the little goals that lead to reaching that overall, big goal. Those little goals are where people find success and gain confidence. Celebrating the little milestones moves people in the right direction and keeps their energy focused on their goal so they can keep building toward it.

Let's say someone's goal is to develop their time-management skills so they increase time efficiency by 10 percent. In the first week, maybe they take a course on Microsoft Outlook. Celebrate that step. Have a milestone moment. Taking this type of action is a great accomplishment. It doesn't matter what milestones you focus on. The point is to reinforce the positive movement along the way. Celebrating that small victory will get them excited that they're accomplishing something, and it will help them dig in more to achieve the bigger goal.

RED ZONE COLLABORATION IN ACTION: DONNA'S DIFFICULTIES

Donna was a senior leader for a large organization. She'd been with the company for years and had moved up through the ranks. She was like Jen, in that she had been the sweetheart of the organization—an up-and-coming star. Now, she was struggling. Her numbers were down, and her markets were suffering. Donna's senior VP asked me to work with Donna to help her turn things around.

Donna was an optimist. When we first sat down together to review the results in the reflect stage of collaboration, she said everything was just great. That was a flag for me because it indicated Donna didn't feel safe enough to be honest with me about what was hurting her. When I coach someone new who doesn't know me, over time and by building the relationship, I can eventually say, "I'm here to help. This is a safe environment for us to talk. What's really going on?" In this case, Donna wasn't ready to trust me.

At one point, she said, "I'm almost up the mountain."

This struck me as a nugget in need of exploring. "Tell me, what does it mean to be 'almost up the mountain?'"

Donna replied, "We're going through a rough time metrics-wise, but we're almost up the mountain. Once we get through a few things, everything will be better."

The story she was telling herself was that the numbers were the result of a rough patch. Once the rough patch was over, everything would be fine again. She and her team needed to keep doing what they were doing, and eventually the problems would go away.

I wanted to help her get back to addressing the real facts instead of accepting the story she had told herself. I asked, "How long have you been going up the mountain?"

"What do you mean?" she asked.

"You said you're almost up the mountain, so how long have you been in this rough patch where everything is so chaotic, where you don't feel like you're able to get the numbers you want?"

She paused for a moment and then said, "Well, I guess it's been a few years."

There was her realization. "It sounds like these problems are not temporary but have been permanent for quite a while now," I said.

"Yes," she agreed.

"What do you think will happen once you're over the mountain?" I asked.

"Well, we'll be able to hit our metrics, and our staffing will get through these transitions and stabilize. Everything will be fine."

I said, "At what point has that ever been the case for you? Or the case for anyone else you know in this organization?"

She paused again and said, "I guess never, actually."

"What makes you think that will eventually happen, if it's never happened before?"

"Well, I have to have hope."

I said, "Yes, but hope's not a strategy. What could you be doing right now to start taking back control so you can get back on track to managing the chaos rather than hoping it will magically go away on its own?"

Now that we'd gotten past the story Donna was telling herself, we could move on to guiding the goal. "Okay," I said. "If you could fix any one thing that's going on, what would you want to fix right now?"

"I would fix my staffing problems."

"Would that be important for us to talk about today?"

"Yes."

"All right, great. By the end of today, you're going to have a strategy to help you reduce the turnover and staffing problems with your field reps. Does that sound right?"

"Yes."

Now we had a one-sentence goal statement that was realistic and specific, so we were ready to move on to rating the reality.

"What are you currently doing to work on staffing problems?" I asked Donna.

"We're doing job fairs, we've got flyers out there, and we've got recruiters looking for talent, but we're not finding quality people."

"Not finding quality people—tell me more about that."

"We're not finding people we'd want to keep."

"Okay. Basically, you're finding people but not the people you want who can do the job?"

"Yes."

This was another nugget for me. She was essentially saying she wasn't finding the right people, which meant she thought the right people existed. She was telling herself a story, that there were perfect, ideal people out there and that she just needed to find them to be successful. I wrote down a note about this so we could come back to it later.

Donna gave me a list of everything they'd been doing to solve this problem, and I had her go through the list and rate each one on a scale of one to ten. She had some sixes, some sevens and eights, and maybe one nine. When she was done, I showed her the list with the corresponding scores and said, "Anything below an eight isn't working. What does that tell us about your current strategy?"

"Wow," she said. "It's not working."

"You're right. It sounds like we need a new strategy and a new plan. Does that work for you?"

"Yes."

I'd heard those key transition words, "It's not working," so we were ready to move on to the explore phase.

"What would be your ideal way of fixing the staffing problem with your field reps?" I asked.

"Having an abundance of people come in and apply," she said.

"All right. Great." At this point, I went back to that nugget I'd noticed earlier about her not finding "quality" people.

"Let me ask you something," I said. "You indicated earlier that you have plenty of people applying, but the problem is you're not having the right people apply. Tell me more about this—who are the right people?"

"Well, I want them to be professional and polished and to show up on time. I want them to have sales skills and be able to hit their metrics so we don't have such high turnover."

This gave me several pieces to begin exploring. "For the people you hire who don't work out, what's causing them to fail?" I asked.

"They're not professional. They don't show up on time, and they're not engaged."

"Why do you think your area has a bigger problem finding the right people than other areas do—people who will show up and who are professional and hit their numbers?"

When I asked this question, Donna realized maybe the problem wasn't the field reps. Maybe it was the leaders doing the hiring. Maybe they weren't looking for the right skills in people. Maybe something they were doing or not doing was causing the problem. As we talked more, it came out that the real issue was not that she had the wrong leaders in place or even that she had the wrong reps in place. The real issue was the onboarding process for new hires. New hires were thrown immediately on the floor and had to engage with customers without any sales training, systems training, or ramp-up time. They were expected to be successful right from the start, despite not having any of the knowledge and training they needed. Eventually, weeks later, they would go through a training process, but by that point, it was no longer relevant. Due to the lack of training, the reps couldn't do the job, couldn't meet the expectations, and they were quickly discouraged. They were being embarrassed in front of customers, and they felt unprofessional. They would stop showing up because they didn't feel as if the company cared about them or was invested in them.

Donna found that rather than trying to find the right people, she might be better off finding the right onboarding process to set new hires up for success. This was the strategy she decided on. She worked with her team to fix the onboarding process so they wouldn't put unrealistic expectations on people and wouldn't put inexperienced people out on the floor before they were ready.

Donna put her plan in place, and I followed up with her a few weeks later. By focusing on the onboarding process, which she could control, new hires were more engaged and more likely to stay. With the proper onboarding process, these new hires were also able to hit their metrics faster and produce better results. The constant turnover disappeared, and her markets were able to catch up and be fully staffed. The problem wasn't finding the right people but finding the right process to help them be effective so they would want to stay and keep working. With the reduced turnover rates and increased sales, her area went back to being one of the top areas in the company.

Donna had been asking the wrong questions and thus getting the wrong answers. Sometimes she hadn't been asking questions at all and just hoping things would get better. The system had been spiraling out of control, but through the RED Zone collaboration process, Donna was able to take a step back and see the story she had been telling herself. She realized, "It's not getting better. We're not almost up the mountain. We're getting worse. What's causing this?" As she explored that question through the collaborative process, she realized it wasn't her people but the onboarding process, and she was able to fix that problem.

Once Donna stopped blaming and started looking at her part in the process—what she could own and control—she was back in the driver's seat. Then things started to turn around. She couldn't control how many people were applying and coming in, but she could control the onboarding process. Once she fixed the onboarding process, she didn't have to fix the number of people coming in because her new hires were staying. People were coming in to a healthier environment and wanted to be there.

PART V CONCLUSION

Although this process can be easy, it's not intuitive. It will take you a little time to shift into this new way of thinking. You just need to practice.

Michael Jordan once said, "I've missed more than nine thousand shots in my career. I've lost almost three hundred games. Twenty-six times I've been trusted to take the game winning shot and missed. I've failed over and over again in my life. And that is why I succeed."[1] You're not going to do this perfectly. You will make mistakes and even fail at times, but if you simply keep practicing, you can make a significant impact.

Too often, we are so afraid to practice, so we never try anything new. We don't like to role-play, and we don't like to make mistakes. We want to do things perfectly right away, and if we can't, then we don't want to do those things at all. But remember Malcolm Gladwell's 10,000-hour rule. Bill Gates succeeded because he put in thousands of hours learning, programming, and practicing. You just need to put in the hours, and you can become a collaboration expert. You may not be a natural at this, but it's not about being a natural. It's about practicing until you become capable. This RED Zone framework is your invitation to practice.

You don't have to be a genius, and you don't have to be a perfect leader, manager, or coach right now to become an effective collaboration coach.

---

1   David L. Andrews, editor, *Michael Jordan, Inc.: Corporate Sport, Media Culture, and Late Modern America* (State University of New York: Albany, 2001), 157.

WHAT IS COLLABORATION?

1. Collaboration is the process of recognizing the power within others and helping them create their own solutions by providing the right awareness, support, and environment to implement change.

2. Collaboration is initiated when a team member/coachee essentially says, "I have a problem. Help me fix myself."

3. In Zone 4, collaboration, the team member/coachee is aware of the coaching need.

4. Collaboration is an effective coaching tool when the team member/coachee has the knowledge to correct their own problem, but they require coaching to help them uncover the true causes and then find the solution within themselves.

5. Through the collaboration process, the leader/coach provides a safe environment and asks questions that allow the team member/coachee to identify and solve their problem.

6. Collaboration assists team members/coachees who need to see a problem clearly, face it, perhaps change their attitude about it, and then determine the best solution.

7. In Zone 4, the leader/coach does not need to be an expert in the specific problems being addressed or potential solutions, but they should be an expert in collaboration coaching.

8. There are two types of collaboration coaching: performance and developmental.

   • In performance coaching, the leader/coach determines the collaboration topics.

   • In developmental coaching, the team member/coachee chooses the topics they want to work on.

9. The team member/coachee always determines the action plan.

PART V QUESTIONS FOR REFLECTION

1. What are the benefits of allowing team members to design their own action plans?

2. Everyone needs a coach to guide and model the behaviors they are trying to learn. Who can you work with that models these collaboration coaching skills that will help you improve your abilities?

3. What steps can you take to improve how you are collaboratively coaching your team?

Part VI

BREAKING THE COACHING CODE

CHAPTER 15

Optimized Coaching

Practice does not make perfect. Only perfect practice makes perfect.

—VINCE LOMBARDI

When all four zones are working together, we call this optimized coaching. Learning each of the four zones is a critical step in becoming a successful coach, but even more important is understanding when to use that zone in the right situation with the right people.

When I was in college, I decided to learn to play tennis. I had a few things going for me. I was young, fast, and healthy. That was about all I had going for me.

My formal training came from going out and playing with friends who knew as much about tennis as I did. The closest to formal training I had was watching Pete Sampras on TV.

One morning, I was hitting practice serves at a local park, and some older gentlemen were warming up for a match. One of them, a guy named Max, asked me if I would like to warm up with him.

Max was over seventy-five years old and walked with a limp. In my youthful arrogance, I thought speed and power were all I needed. What was this old geezer going to teach me?

Within five minutes, Max demonstrated to me the power of technique. He was able to place the ball anywhere on the court he wanted. He had me running from one side to the other chasing after the ball—with little success. When I was able to make contact with the ball, I didn't return it with the unusual spin Max so effortlessly applied. This elder gentleman, who could barely walk across the court, dominated the game by using the right technique at the right time.

Years later, that lesson I learned on the tennis court that day still rings true, in the tennis court and many other places too. I learned you don't have to be able to run like a twenty-year-old or have the power serve of Sampras to be a successful tennis player. In fact, using the right technique at the right time meant I didn't have to run as much or depend on one style of serving. Over the years, I have matured. I don't go out and play as hard as I can. I have learned to play smart. I found that control over the ball means I can win against people half my age and ability. Accuracy is more important than speed. Knowing what to do on the court and when to do it were paramount. The same is true in coaching.

The best coaches know how to use the right tool in the right situation to move performance in others.

Optimized coaching is the ability to apply each of the four zones at the right moments to maximize your results. By utilizing the right zone for each coaching opportunity, you will increase your accuracy, achieve the desired result, and do it more quickly.

Coaching is a concept that few leaders truly understand and even fewer know how to effectively use. Many managers scrape by, using one or two methods. They learn enough to get by but never master all the zones and learn when and how to apply them to improve performance and transform their teams.

NO MORE EXCUSES

When I ask leaders why they don't utilize coaching more, I often hear things like, "It requires too much time and effort." Others say, "You have to go to specialized trainings and have certifications. These things take time I don't have and money I can't spend." Even when companies provide training and resources for coaching and people attend, the implementation doesn't seem to stick. I would argue that many leaders fail to adopt coaching not because of the time and resources but rather due to the coach's mindset.

Let's revisit my tennis example. When I decided to take up tennis, I committed an enormous amount of time and money to the game. I bought the best racket I could afford. I invested in new shoes to improve my performance and used new tennis balls. I committed many hours to the game, getting out to play with my friends every free moment. Max, on the other hand, spent nowhere near as much time as I was on the game. He didn't have the best shoes, nor was his racket the latest and greatest. He had limited physical ability and time to be on the court. However, the time he spent was focused on very specific techniques that greatly improved his game. Some may argue that Max put the time in over the years and that is what made his performance exceptional, and I would agree—to a certain point. But here's the difference between me and Max: he spent his time practicing the right things.

If I kept working hard doing what I was doing, I would see only minimal growth years later. I'd still be climbing that mountain, so to speak, and never reaching the top. By changing the way I practiced and played the game, I drastically improved my performance.

After meeting Max, I started working with a tennis coach. Through that coaching relationship, I learned that tennis was not only about running as fast as I could and hitting the ball as hard as I was able. I learned how to control my shots and ultimately win games.

THE WINNABLE GAME

I am not sure I would still play tennis today if I hadn't lost to Max that day. Up until that point, when I lost at tennis, I tended to blame things like my shoes, the tennis court, and my racket. I would blame anything if it provided me with an excuse as to why I consistently lost. I thought the tools were faulty. After playing Max, I realized I had a bigger problem. My thinking was faulty. I wasn't focusing on the one thing that could make the game winnable: me. I never underestimate the importance of winning. The game has to be winnable.

I think many would-be coaches give up because they don't see an immediate return on investment for the time and effort they put into coaching. They work hard and then realize they don't have a winning formula and they give up.

Just the other day, I observed a coach providing coaching tips and methods to an audience of municipal employees. He gave them more than fifty principles and points in a matter of three hours. This massive information dump was over-whelming for me personally to take in, and I'm a coach. I couldn't imagine what someone hearing topics like this for the first time was feeling. Since I wasn't coaching, I observed the participants. One after another, they stopped taking notes and pushed their workbooks away. After about thirty minutes, they were all pretty much disengaged. Many people folded their arms and left them that way until the end of the session. They didn't say it aloud, but it was clear they had given up. It was useful content, yet it overloaded the audience. It was as if I could hear participants all over the room go, "I'm out!" with their actions.

The coach thought he was doing a fantastic job. After all, he'd presented oodles of great content. What else did people expect?

ACTION IS NOT ACHIEVEMENT

We should never mistake actions for achievement. Just because I was busy playing tennis doesn't mean I was achieving my tennis goals. Likewise, just because that coach was dumping all kinds of coaching tips on the participants doesn't mean he was coaching them or helping them to learn in any way or improve their performance or results. This is a winnable game, but you must figure out the right things to do and spend your time doing them.

Managers and team members spend a great deal of time doing things every day, but are those things producing results? It wasn't until I started my own business that this became real to me. When I worked in the corporate world,

I could fill an entire day with meetings, calls, and emails. I would go home feeling exhausted, thinking I had done so much. I believed that because I was busy, I had made an impact for the company. When I started my own company, no matter how many meetings, calls, or emails I completed for the day, I had to ask myself, "Did I produce results?" I could fill a day doing things. The problem wasn't finding things to do but doing the right things that generated revenue and growth.

Focusing on the right things reduces the amount of time and energy it takes to produce results. This starts by understanding the coaching zones and learning when and how to apply each one. By becoming proficient at all four coaching zones and by knowing how to use them, leaders can optimize their performance and impact. You don't have to master each step right away. Just learn the basics. Then, practice those basics over and over. Mastery will come in due time.

CHAPTER 16

MAPS

Maps encourage boldness. They're like cryptic love letters. They make anything seem possible.

—MARK JENKINS

Before smartphones, Xbox, and home computers, kids played a lot of sports. Not the formal team sports kids play today, but informal, neighborhood games that broke out after school, on weekends, and during summer breaks. Kids wandered out of their houses and gathered in the middle of the street or at a local park. All you needed was a ball and a few kids eager to play. The best player would take the role of quarterback and call plays, and most of these plays were organized chaos at best. In the huddle, it sounded like this: "Okay everyone, go out and get open." Inevitably someone would get open and we would move the ball down the field.

This strategy worked for a game of street football, but you wouldn't expect a pro team to run their plays the same way.

Surprisingly, organizations employ tactics like the preteen quarterbacks from my childhood. The leadership team gets a bright idea and, at the last minute, calls for everyone to drop what they're doing and get open to make their play happen. In the corporate world, team members call this "the flavor of the month." Many of these impulsive strategies die before they ever complete, often because the leadership team would call another play. Again, everyone was expected to drop what they were doing and commit all their attention and resources to the latest flavor of the month, week, or day. Employees eventually learned to ride out these waves of strategic chaos, knowing they were short-lived and would likely be interrupted with a new play.

As an outside coach and consultant, I'm shocked to see how many organizations manage day-to-day operations this way. After observing the phenomenon—because I can't even call it a strategy or a plan—enough times, I discovered the heart of the problem. This was the only play many leaders knew how to run. Over time, this management style had become a core part of the culture. Organized chaos plays were taught to future leaders and new managers—passed down like some kind of twisted legacy—as the appropriate way to run their teams. As this way of thinking permeated throughout the organization, it created the corporate vortex we discussed in previous chapters.

PAUL'S PARADIGM

Paul was new to the organization and hired into a management role. In his previous company, he'd had some impressive career wins and was next in line for a senior level position. However, after an unexpected change in his family situation, Paul had to move to a new city, which meant taking a new job at this new company.

Paul walked into his new role with grand expectations for his team. He had heard about their drive and ability to get things done, but after spending some time observing the group, Paul realized they were active—in fact, the room was a flurry of activity—but they accomplished little. At the end of the day, there wasn't much getting done.

He pulled one member, a young staffer named David, aside and asked him how the team managed their jobs. What were their goals and objectives, and how was the work prioritized? David explained how the organization worked.

"We have 'fire drills' each month where we rush around getting new materials out to all our clients, and we have calls with the key people there. We visit a number of clients and have meetings with them, then we have more meetings when we get back to the office."

Paul asked, "How many of these visits help you reach your targets or drive revenue?"

David stared, unable to answer the question.

Paul continued, "How many of these fire drills—and the meetings—could be avoided with proper planning?"

David didn't have an answer for that either, and neither did anyone else on the team. It was how they did business, and no one dared question it or attempt to buck the system.

When Paul confronted his team about why they seemed so busy yet weren't meeting their goals, he heard a lot of excuses, and they all pointed to other people. Clients weren't buying because of their poor product line. Leadership didn't motivate or incentivize them enough. Competition offered sharp discounts. What were they supposed to do about these problems which were all beyond their control?

Paul decided to try a new play with the team, one that focused on working from the inside out. It challenged the team to think differently in how they approached their jobs and clients. Instead of putting more hours in each week, he wanted them to think carefully about what they were accomplishing in the time they spent doing their day-to-day tasks, calls, meetings, and everything else that consumed their workday.

Paul said, "Before we attempt to go out and fix our client issues, let's fix the ones right in front of us."

That young staffer on Paul's team, David, was me. Working with Paul changed the way I looked at business and ultimately led me to develop a new coaching strategy.

Organized chaos worked just fine for street football, but successful coaching required maps.

A NEW STRATEGY: MAPS

I call this strategy MAPS: Mindset, Attitude, Plan, Situation. Over the years, I've worked with corporate leaders to incorporate the four aspects of MAPS into their coaching strategies. MAPS sets the stage for better coaching with an approach that benefits the coach and the coachee. It encourages introspection, dignity, and respect to coaching so everyone involved can enjoy a more positive experience while reaping the benefits of a purposeful process.

MAPS uses an inside-out approach, working with the people first, rather than focusing on the problem. Employ all four steps of MAPS for the best results.

MINDSET

Change the way you look at things, and the things you look at change.[1]

—DR. WAYNE W. DYER

---

[1] Wayne W. Dyer, "Success Secrets," *Wayne's Blog*, accessed March 25, 2018, https://www.drwaynedyer.com/blog/success-secrets.

Mindset is a critical aspect of coaching. What you bring, mentally to a coaching session—what you think will happen—determines what does happen. If you attend a coaching session with your mind made up that an employee isn't going to make it on your team, your mindset becomes a self-fulfilling prophecy for what takes place in the meeting. You will, consciously or unconsciously, guide the meeting in the direction of getting rid of that individual. Far too often, managers go through the motions of these required "coaching sessions" that are really a prelude to termination. In many cases, there is nothing a team member can do to change the direction of the coaching session since the leader's mind is made up.

Malcolm and the Mistaken Mindset

Malcolm, a manager, was underperforming. His team continued to miss their targets each month. Although there were some legitimate reasons for not hitting the targets, senior leaders decided that Malcolm needed to go. Instead of coaching Malcolm to help him improve, they put him on boot-camp calls with other underperformers, thinking these calls would motivate him to improve performance. Occasionally, Malcolm would receive a call from the EVP voicing his concern for his team's underperformance.

Senior leadership eventually decided that Malcolm was not the right fit and needed to be worked out of the organization.

For the next few months, his replacement was brought in and masked in another role so they could work alongside Malcolm and learn the job.

At the time, I was working as a consultant and helping with some projects in the organization. Malcolm, frustrated with his situation, reached out to me for some feedback. He said, "David, I think they're trying to get rid of me." All the evidence supported this deduction, and I wanted to say, "Yes, and you would be well served to get your resume updated." In fact, I had heard through the leadership channels that the decision had been made months earlier to make changes in his division. They were using passive-aggressive methods to send the message, hoping he would get the point and quit. If that didn't work, they would eventually move to counseling statements to justify their decision and would eventually terminate him. This was their typical way of working out their problems.

Malcolm wanted to stay. He wanted to fight for his position. He was a good manager historically but wasn't sure how to change the minds of the people making the decisions. What leadership had overlooked was that Malcolm's performance had rebounded and his numbers were on the rise. They had already made up their minds, though, and were blind to his recent successes. Instead, they dismissed it as a temporary fluke and continued down the path of termination. Fortunately for Malcolm, he found a position at another organization and left the company before they could fire him.

Leaders often see what they want to see in team members, the good and the bad. A manager might have a team member whom they believe can do no wrong. Others on the team wonder why nothing is ever said or done about certain individuals and their destructive behaviors, yet the leader appears oblivious. Psychologists call this the "halo effect," and there is a "horns effect" as well, which is just the opposite: they see only the negative in certain people. As a leader, the outcome you expect, which may be heavily influenced by the way you view a person, is the outcome you will get.

Whatever the leader has decided about the person will dictate the outcome in the coaching session.

When you think about your team members, what have you already decided about everyone, and how might it affect your ability to coach them to growth? Are you their limitation? On the other hand, do you have team members you continue to give a pass to for underperformance or inappropriate behaviors? What excuses do you continue to make so you don't have to coach them to growth?

The most critical point is, as the leader and coach, you are in the driver's seat of helping your team grow or not grow. No one has the power you hold, the ability to choose the destination, put it in the GPS, and determine the direction your coaching will take. No one has more influence and control over driving the team than you do. It all begins with what you have decided about your team and what can be possible.

Mindset can be described many ways, but for the purposes of MAPS, think of mindset this way: your mindset is how you perceive and think about the world around you.

Think about it this way. When you get in your car, your windshield provides a view of the world outside the car. Your windshield might be dirty or sparkling clean, and even though it's the same windshield either way, a dirty windshield impairs your view, your driving, and your decisions.

In a coaching relationship, there are two mindsets to consider: that of the coach and that of the coachee. If the coach doesn't have the correct mindset, then the coaching will be doomed before it begins. The coachee mindset is equally important because they need to feel there is hope and a clear path to change.

Two practical steps can help you shift your mindset and optimize the coaching experience.

Shift the Body to Shift the Mind

The first step is simple: to shift the mind, shift the body. Social psychologist Amy Cuddy discusses, in her TED Talk and in her book *Presence*, how to change your mindset by changing your physical body. Her research explored this key question. We know the mind changes the body, but can the body change the mind? In her book, Cuddy suggests that not only does body language affect the way others perceive us, but more so, our body language affects the way we perceive ourselves. She and a colleague conducted a study where participants' testosterone and cortisol levels were tested prior to doing different assigned poses for two minutes. Some in the study were asked to do what she refers to as "power poses," such as the Superman pose with your hands on your hips, kicking your feet up on a table or desk, and stretching your hands up and out in victory, as if you've just won a race. Other participants were asked to hold poses associated with insecurity and fear: hunched over in a chair, legs crossed, arms crossed, or sitting in a way to make them feel smaller.

After two minutes, the testosterone and cortisol levels were checked again. According to the study, the people who had completed power poses increased their testosterone and lowered their cortisol levels. These individuals were more likely to take risks and handle stress better. They also felt they were more likely to win and had an optimistic view to approaching people and situations. Those who had not done power poses had different results: their testosterone went down, and cortisol went up. Their stress levels went up and they were less likely to take risks. These people, who had held poses associated with insecurity and fear, did not feel as optimistic about winning.

They did this same experiment with individuals preparing to go on a job interview. The interviewers were instructed to not provide any emotion to the interviewees' responses. These interviews were recorded, and outsider coders were asked to watch the recorded interviews without knowing the conditions of the study. They were asked to select the candidates to hire. In every case, the coders selected the people who had done the power poses over those who had done the insecure poses.[2]

The most powerful part of this study to me is that it took only two minutes to change the person's mindset. By changing our bodies, we begin to shift our minds. I am not suggesting you take this one study to an extreme or that you go around kicking your feet up on tables during meetings. I am suggesting you take the foundational principles to heart. If you want to shift the mind, take a few moments to evaluate how you are carrying your body, especially when you are coaching others. Where do you sit? How do you sit? What is your posture like? Do you fidget or become easily distracted? Are you loud and overbearing, and do you hover over the person while they sit at their desk?

Move Your Body, Move Your Mindset

Another question to ask yourself is, "Do you coach with

---

2   Amy Cuddy, *Presence: Bringing Your Boldest Self to Your Biggest Challenges* (New York: Hachette, 2015), 199–206.

barriers between you and the coachee (i.e., like having a table or desk in-between you)?"

I worked with a senior VP who sat in different locations in her own office, depending on how she wanted to approach a meeting. When she was open to discussions and dialogue, she would come around her desk and sit beside the other person at a small table in her office. With this small move, her posture and her tone changed. On the other hand, if she was not open to change, she remained behind her large mahogany desk. Her tone was sharp, and she would be more combative in her approach to the discussion. In most cases, the result when she was behind her desk was a predetermined solution she had decided beforehand. I learned to schedule meetings with this VP away from her office in a conference room or breakroom. This shifted her mindset and mine, and altered our interactions. By simply changing our physical location, where we coach and how we present ourselves, we can open up a whole new discussion in ourselves and others.

Beware of Negative Bias

Be aware of your beliefs about the person you're coaching and how it affects your approach to coaching. Also, be aware of a negative bias, which could make the coachee perceive you and coaching in a very different way than you intended.

Negativity is part of our chemical makeup for survival, and

we tend to see the world as a dog-eat-dog place with lots of problems. Think about the number of news stories and articles that focus on the negative. We're attracted to articles that offer the scoop on the latest celebrity divorce or financial ruin of a millionaire more than the latest hero that provided aid to hurricane victims. Because of this human tendency, when we approach coaching opportunities with others, they often hear only the negative. Recall from Chapter 7 that it takes five positive comments to balance one negative one.

Managers are often unaware of this balance, and either focus too much on the negative or avoid addressing problems at all. Understand and use the knowledge of the negative bias when coaching to your advantage, and to the advantage of the team member. You'll get better results addressing a situation from a positive perspective than by simply attacking the negative behaviors.

Piper's Plight

For example, I was working with a general manager of a real estate company. Some of her staff was subcontracted from a unionized company, and she was struggling to manage one individual. Piper wanted to coach him, and I asked her what her goal was for the coaching session.

Without hesitation, she said, "I want this employee to stop

using his headphones, sit up straight at the desk, and memorize every customer's name as they enter the building."

I then asked her what she ultimately wanted from this employee. Piper simply repeated the same list of desired behaviors.

I said, "Putting aside this one employee, what would you like their role to demonstrate?"

She said, "I want us to be a world-class organization."

"So, your goal is for this employee to model the behaviors of a world-class residential community."

She said, "Yes!"

I wanted Piper to see that she could try to coach to the negative behaviors of the employee, but that may not fix the bigger concern. Even if he stopped using headphones at work and ignoring residents and succeeded in memorizing everyone's name, he still may not represent Piper's vision of a world-class company. However, if she coached the employee with the goal of representing a world-class organization and invited him into the process of what that would look like and how to create it, he might respond radically different.

Piper learned that if she coached to the positive, the other negative behaviors went away. Once he started partnering with her to create a world-class community, the employee adopted new behaviors that he believed represented the business the way they both envisioned it, and part of that was not wearing headphones, paying attention to customers, and greeting everyone by name.

MINDSET QUESTIONS FOR REFLECTION

Now that you understand how mindset affects coaching, ask yourself the following questions:

- How am I approaching the individual I am coaching?

- What's their potential?

- What outcome do I want in this situation?

- How can I shift my mindset toward the situation and the person?

- What do I believe about this person?

- What kind of person could they be if they were given the right tools and resources to succeed?

ATTITUDE

The greatest discovery of my generation is that human beings can alter their lives by altering their attitudes of mind.

—WILLIAM JAMES, PSYCHOLOGIST

You learned in the previous section how mindset affects

our thoughts about a situation. Attitude, the second part of MAPS, affects our feelings and prepares our thoughts for change. Though attitude is fundamental to coaching, it's a bit like the wind: you don't really see the wind, but you see evidence of it. You can't really see attitude, but you can see symptoms of attitude. If a leader tells a team member they have an attitude problem, the team member can simply say they don't, and—aside from pointing to symptoms as evidence—there's no way to prove which of them is correct.

People are emotional beings, and when we're put into a situation we don't know how to deal with, our bodies respond with a fight-or-flight response. Whenever you feel pressure, stress, or frustration, which are constant feelings for many people, the fight-or-flight response is triggered. When you're in the heat of the moment, when you're emotional and unsure about what to do, your blood goes from your higher brain functions to your lower brain functions, extremities, and heart. Your body prepares to either run away from whatever is threatening you or to fight. The problem is, your higher brain function shuts down in this physical state.

I call people in this state "emotionally hooked." They're upset, frustrated, angry, and stuck in fight-or-flight mode, unable to unhook themselves from those emotions. When I encounter someone stuck in this state, I'll sometimes ask, "Hey, by the way, what's five plus five?" At first, they'll give me some weird number, like eighteen. I know their math skills are better than that, and I ask again. This time they'll answer ten. I can almost see the blood rushing back to their head as they start thinking logically again.

Being aware of your attitude as you approach coaching is critical because the people who know you best—your family members, close friends, and your team—know what to do or say to push your buttons and cause an emotional reaction. Sometimes the person you're coaching will push your buttons to deflect the situation. If you're trying to walk someone through a process, they might try to throw you off and shift the focus away from what it should be, which is them. For example, if you're addressing a team member's issue with being late, they might respond with "Well, you're late sometimes. Maybe you should fix yourself before you talk to me about being late," or "Oh, you want to talk to me about being late? Susie over here, she's the one that's late all the time. You need to deal with her before you talk to me. I'm only a few minutes late. She's got the real problem."

When you find yourself emotionally hooked due to a team member's deflections or for any other reason, be aware of your attitude, adjust it, and reengage.

The first step to working on attitude is recognizing when you're hooked. Then, slow down, step out of the situation, and focus on something else that allows you to regain your composure and think logically instead of allowing your emotions to take over. You could listen to some music, go for a walk, call a friend, write in a journal, play with a puppy, read a book, or meditate. Everyone is different and has their own way to unhook. Your personal method isn't important, but it is important to know how to unhook yourself and reengage with a positive attitude. If you go into a situation scared, nervous, or angry, you won't be emotionally ready to have a quality coaching session, so find an activity that allows you to return to an emotionally neutral place.

The main struggle with attitude is that it can change quickly. You can prepare for coaching with a good mindset and attitude, knowing what you want to accomplish and feeling good about it. You start with a great attitude, but a team member says or does something to invoke an emotional reaction from you, and suddenly, you're hooked. As a leader, you need to unhook yourself before you can provide an effective coaching session.

When two people become hooked, there is no possibility for a positive outcome until they disengage from the emotional situation and think logically. In this situation, you might say or do things out of character that don't reflect your true self. Think about a conversation you had with a person where you were emotionally hooked and said something to hurt them. You regret those words, but you can prevent yourself from saying them in the first place if you train yourself to recognize when you're emotionally hooked and step away from the situation. Taking that step back can be tough because people tend to want to prove their point in the heat of the moment. However, you need to think logically to consider your objective and responsibility in the discussion and move forward productively.

If you get into this type of situation, stop the coaching session and take steps to reset your attitude before you continue.

ATTITUDE QUESTIONS FOR REFLECTION

Now that you understand how attitude affects coaching, ask yourself the following questions:

- What negative attitudes are hurting you and your team currently?

- What steps can you take to reengage your mind when you become emotionally hooked?

- What beliefs are limiting your team from operating at their full potential?

PLAN

It had long since come to my attention that people of accomplishment rarely sat back and let things happen to them. They went out and happened to things.

—LEONARDO DA VINCI

Millions of people...falsely believe that 'knowledge is power.' It is nothing of the sort! Knowledge is only potential power. It becomes power only when, and if, it is organized into definite plans of action and directed to a definite end.

—NAPOLEON HILL, *THINK AND GROW RICH!*

These quotes emphasize the importance of having a plan. Everything has potential, but it's the direction you give things—your plan—that makes them powerful.

We have talked at length in other chapters about the process of planning, but I want to reemphasize the importance of planning prior to a coaching session. You can have the right mindset and the best attitude, but if you fail to plan, your coaching session is a crapshoot.

Getting in a car without knowing where you're going or how to get there is pointless, but that's exactly how people often approach coaching. They expect to get together and figure out coaching without first asking themselves what they're trying to accomplish and how they plan to accomplish it. That strategy is not an effective tool to maximize a coaching moment. Whether you're coaching with feedback, training, mentoring, or collaboration, you need a clear plan before you begin. Knowing what you are trying to accomplish gives you focus.

With that said, when you have a plan as you begin coaching an individual, you should remain flexible. Think of it this way: if your GPS is navigating you toward your destination, things may come up along the way that require you to correct your course. There will be construction zones, traffic, accidents, and other obstacles. You may need to take a moment to recalibrate. Have a plan, but be flexible so as you get additional information, you can make changes to the plan. Instead of barreling through the obstacles, you may have to rethink your plan and take a detour. With new information, your goals and strategies for achieving them might change. Sometimes you'll approach a situation with a bad plan because you don't have enough information, so being adaptable, flexible, and open to looking at the situation in a different way is critical.

Scott's Surprise

Scott, a participant in a coaching course for senior leaders, approached me during a break. "David," he said, "I have a problem. One of my employees, John, has worked for me for three years. He was outstanding in the past but hasn't been performing well during the last six months. I feel like he doesn't want to work for us anymore. He's late to work all the time and doesn't make his deliverables. I've tried coaching him, but he's not getting any better. In fact, I've reached out to HR to talk about ways to get rid of him."

I asked Scott about the specifics of the issues. How many times had John been late, and which specific deliverables had he failed to make? Like many leaders who have become frustrated with employees and their behaviors, Scott didn't have the answers. His tendency was to simply ignore the problem until it became so bad that he would explode into action. Once leaders reach this point, they tend to go to extreme measures to correct problems that could have been corrected easily along the way.

Scott acknowledged that most of his coaching with John revolved around offering recommendations and potential solutions to correct his tardiness issue. He offered time-management techniques, recommended he get a new alarm clock, and even offered to help him explore alternative ways to get to the office. Although Scott was trying to be helpful, he missed the heart of the problem. He was using a shotgun method to address an important issue, spraying solutions and hoping one of them would hit the target and make the problem go away. Scott lacked a clear plan and process to get to the heart of the problem.

Once the training was over for the day, Scott—now armed with a better plan and process—decided to address this issue with John differently. First, he had to discover the facts of the matter before he spoke to John again. Then, he would step John through the collaboration coaching process.

The next day, Scott showed up early to my coaching course before anyone else arrived. He pulled me aside and said,

"I need to talk to you about something. It's John. I'm so embarrassed."

Scott told me he had followed my instructions, documenting the details of John's behavior and performance and then meeting with John that morning to begin the collaboration process.

"Well, I started off with the facts: how often John was late and how much his performance was off. I asked him to explain his side of the story. At first, he gave me more excuses, but as I continued to ask questions, he finally shared what was happening behind the scenes. He said, 'You want to know what's really going on? My wife has cancer. I have to take her to chemotherapy every morning, and that's why I'm late. I feel like I'm being pulled between being a good employee and being a dedicated husband, and it feels like I'm not doing either one very well.'"

Scott had been completely unaware of John's real issue, but once he had this new knowledge, his plan for coaching John began to change. I was relieved to hear the coaching session brought these important facts to light, but I didn't understand why Scott was embarrassed.

"I was embarrassed because I never took the time to ask the right questions and address the real concerns going on in John's life. I was so busy doing my job that I wasn't doing the right job of supporting my team. If I had approached John sooner, he and I could have talked about this a long time ago. The company could have made changes to better support him."

After this conversation, the company adjusted John's schedule, so he could make his chemo appointments with his wife. He was soon back on track with his work. John was an experienced high performer who had been with the company three years, but they had been prepared to let him go over a misunderstanding that was cleared up with a single conversation. With a coaching plan and a willingness to change the plan based on additional information, Scott prevented the company from making that mistake.

Leaders can be too eager to get rid of people instead of asking questions to find out what they need. Employees are people, and like most people, they have a lot going on in their lives. Shift happens, and unexpected events—like divorce, or cancer—must be adjusted for.

When addressing issues with your team, put yourself in their shoes and be the leader you would want to work for. As a leader, it's up to you to model the behaviors you want to see in your people because you are their role model and example of how to lead. Celebrate the wins and coach the losses. Real superheroes don't save others; they teach others to save themselves.

PLAN QUESTIONS FOR REFLECTION

Now that you understand how planning affects coaching, ask yourself the following questions:

- How has poor planning in the coaching process affected your team and their ability to perform effectively?

- What behaviors are you currently ignoring that are eventually going to lead to an explosive response to how you address your team members?

- What steps do you need to take to create a plan that will help you and the people you coach make positive change?

SITUATION

"A relationship without trust is like having a phone with no service. And what do you do with a phone with no service? You play games."

—ANONYMOUS

The situation part of MAPS is about creating a safe place for coaching to take place. Create an environment that fosters coaching, establish trust, and provide coaching at the right time. Recall Camila's story from Chapter 13 and how I ensured a safe environment for our developmental collaboration coaching sessions. If I had not protected Camila's privacy and gained her trust, she would not have felt comfortable telling me about her personal issues and how they were affecting her performance.

Safety

It's easy to miss the mark when creating a safe environment because we simply don't think about it, and it's not a high priority in our coaching plan. Many years ago, while I was in college, I drove a bus. I was a terrible bus driver because safety wasn't my number one priority. Instead, I was more concerned with getting people from point A to point B as quickly as possible. The job paid the same no matter how long it took to accomplish that goal, so I didn't focus on safety but on speed.

The faster I drove, the sooner I finished, so I drove at the speed of light to unload the bus. Focusing on that goal jeopardized the safety of the passengers.

It's the same with coaching: safety must be your number one priority. Safety happens by design, not by chance. Whether it's driving a bus or coaching an individual, you can't expect safety to be part of the situation unless you make a concerted effort to consider it and include it within the coaching environment.

Environment

Provide safety by delivering your coaching conversations in an appropriate environment. This means not always doing what's easy or convenient in the short term but taking more time for better results in the long term.

Emma's Embarrassment

As an example, I stopped in a coffee shop between appointments one day and overheard a conversation between a manager and one of the employees, Emma. I could tell by the manager's tone of voice and body language that he was in a hurry. He probably had many other tasks to take care of that day and was squeezing in this serious conversation with the woman in front of her coworkers and customers.

He started out with pleasantries but quickly shifted gears and cut to the chase. I heard him say, "Here's what you're having a problem with, Emma." He listed all her problems with coworkers and customers. Of course, the workers and customers were all standing around, spectators to the conversation.

The manager went on to say, "I used to have a problem like this, and here's how I fixed it." Then, he told Emma what to do about her relationships with the people who worked there and came in for coffee. Emma sat there and didn't utter a word. She was too embarrassed and unable to defend herself or even vocalize her side of the conversation, given the audience. She finally began to speak defensively, but quickly realized she was embarrassing herself further and digging a hole with the manager and everyone within earshot, so she simply agreed to follow his advice.

This uncomfortable conversation lasted about fifteen minutes, and the manager probably felt he could check that task off his to-do list. However, Emma probably did not change her behaviors, and now knowing she couldn't trust her coworkers and wasn't working in a safe environment, she may have quit.

That interaction and the corresponding results would have been different if the manager had considered the coaching environment. He could have taken Emma outside or to another location, away from her coworkers and customers, where she felt safer and not at risk of humiliation. Once he'd established a safe environment, he could have asked better questions to understand how she felt her relationships with her team members and customers was going. Instead of fifteen minutes, that conversation might have taken thirty minutes, but it would have allowed Emma to express herself and come to the same conclusion that he had. If she'd been coached in an environment where she could come to the conclusion herself, she would have been more open to accepting the issue and taking responsibility to correct it. That coaching situation was destined to fail from the start because the manager didn't make safety his number one priority.

Consider the Conversation

The proper environment for a coaching conversation can change, depending on the conversation. For example, if the manager had been praising the employee, the public setting wouldn't have mattered as much. You can coach in your office or on the floor with your staff. Evaluate each situation on a case-by-case basis, then ask yourself, "What's the right place and time to have this conversation to make sure it's safe?"

Besides determining the environment for the conversation, you also should consider what you need to have within that environment to make it safe. For example, having a box of tissues can make an environment safer. If you're discussing something emotional and getting to the heart of an issue, people sometimes get upset. If someone starts crying, they need to be able to blow their nose or wipe off runny makeup, so having the tissues available creates safety.

As we discussed in the mindset section of MAPS, your physical positioning and how you engage with people also affects feelings of safety. If you stand over someone or talk to them across a desk, that person feels less safe than if the two of you sit together in chairs. This doesn't mean you have to have all your conversations sitting next to people. There's a time and place to have conversations standing up or looking over a desk. You need to evaluate the situation to determine what level of safety is required. Once you have an idea of how much safety you need, decide who should sit closest to the door, whether the windows should be open, or whether someone else should be in the room. These are all elements that can impact the safety of a coaching environment.

Distractions also affect the environment. If your phone beeps, if people are walking in and out of your office, or if you're constantly looking at your computer screen or doing email, those interruptions and distractions might seem harmless, but they create a very unsafe environment for the person you're coaching. People are so used to the daily distractions of technology that they usually don't consider how offensive it can be to someone on the receiving end of a coaching situation.

Body language and verbal cues play an important part in conversations. Eye contact, nodding, having your body turned toward or away from a person, and occasional comments to let them know you're listening affect how they perceive your level of interest. No one wants to talk to an inattentive, uninterested audience.

Trust

In addition to the environment, you must be a trustworthy leader who's built trusting relationships with the people you coach. Different forms of coaching require different levels of trust.

Have you ever been in an environment where you didn't trust the person managing you or coaching you? How likely were you to give them information about what was really going on with you? If you don't trust someone, you won't share with them. You stick to superficial topics and conversations and avoid being vulnerable. You might even be afraid they'll use any information you give them against you so you don't tell them what they need to hear.

Increasing a person's trust in you is quite simple: do what you say you're going to do. Follow up. Be authentic. If you have an agenda, be upfront about it. Vulnerability is critical to establishing trust. Most importantly, be trustworthy consistently. You can't be trustworthy in just one situation and expect someone to trust you. You must demonstrate a pattern of trustworthiness.

Ask yourself how trustworthy you are. Would you trust a person like you with your most valuable secrets? What would a person like you do with those secrets? Would they keep them or barter or negotiate with that information? If you wouldn't trust someone like you, how can you expect others to trust you?

Too often, people think trust happens because of position. They think a team member should trust them simply because they're the boss. It's behaviors and relationships, not position, that make trust possible. To become more trustworthy, don't violate anyone's trust. Trust isn't just about what you do and say with people you coach but also what you do and say about others around those people. If you talk behind someone's back to people, those people will know you probably talk about them in the same way to others. Leaders often think they can share certain information about people because they're leaders. They might tell themselves it's good for others to know, but they're only humiliating people, undermining their process of growth and creating distrust.

An important principle here is to protect and defend people when they are not present. How much sharing needs to happen about confidential coaching information with others outside of the coaching relationship? When does this sharing cross over to gossip or venting? In many cases, trust is not violated in the serious issues. It's violated around the trivial things. Small compromises in character or little discrepancies in integrity make us question the big ones.

Repairing Trust

What happens when trust has been violated? You can't confront issues, train people, or provide coaching until you first repair broken trust. In most cases, the best tool to repair relationships is often the simplest one: apologize. Own your mistakes in the situation and acknowledge where you have failed. A sincere apology can go a long way in reestablishing trust.

In my youth, I used to think I needed to prove I was right to everyone. There were many cases where my point or opinion was correct, but how I handled the situation was totally wrong. I learned that building a relationship with others was not about proving my opinions but respecting and honoring others. Today, I am quick to apologize, not because my facts are wrong but because of how I handled the facts. I have learned that the relationship is much more important than winning the argument. Although I continue to have to work on this within myself, I have accepted the reality that mistakes are inevitable. Failure is going to happen, but how I own and acknowledge those mistakes define me more as a leader, a father, a husband, and a friend than simply trying to avoid all mistakes and hiding my frailties from others.

Your people are more likely to trust an authentically flawed leader than one who walks around guarded and unable to own their failures in a situation. My respect is far greater for a manager who takes responsibility for their team and actions than one who blames others for why they failed to achieve their targets or the way they performed. We want to be the perfect leader, but we tend to trust the honest ones, and the ones we can relate to, flaws and all.

It's all right to be broken in the right places. In the horse world, we hear the term "breaking in a horse." It refers to breaking a green horse in so it can be ridden. Watching this process done correctly is a beautiful experience. It doesn't have to be about hurting and forcing an animal into submission, even though some try this approach. However, it can be an opportunity for the horse and rider to learn to build a partnership of trust and bonding. The horse must give up some of its control, and so must the rider. Both learn to address their fears and vulnerabilities. Eventually, what emerges is a highly rewarding partnership.

Timeliness

Timeliness is about having a coaching conversation at the right time. Coaching fails most often because it doesn't happen at all or because it doesn't happen at the right time. When leaders get emotionally hooked, they want to have a coaching conversation right away to fix the problem. They don't slow down and do the MAPS work that allows them to reengage their logical brain. Remember, the MAPS process isn't necessarily for the coachee but for the coach to approach the situation in a better, more authentic way that helps them have a better plan and speak to the real situation.

Timeliness is about slowing down and making sure coaching occurs at the right time. Sometimes issues are addressed too late. For example, a leader may pull someone aside to discuss something that happened months ago and is no longer relevant. When that happens, the coaching just hurts the relationship between coach and coachee because the issue wasn't addressed when it mattered.

The Humongous Hot-Head

Issues can also be addressed too early. While I was working on a coaching project with a manager and a director, we visited one of their retail stores. I overheard a representative on the floor giving a customer incorrect information, so I turned to the manager, who was a bear of a man at six-foot-eight and asked whether he'd heard the exchange. I meant to point it out as something that might need to be corrected later, but he decided to fix it immediately. The manager went over to this five-foot-six representative, and towering over her, said in front of the customer, the director, and everybody else, "I need to see you in the back right now." He pulled the representative off the floor, and they had a yelling match in the back room.

When the rep and the manager came back out, they were both highly distressed. Of course, the director now had to have a tough conversation with the manager. Why in the world had he chosen that moment, in front of the rep's customer and coworkers, to address the problem? Nothing good came out of this situation, and in fact, the coaching made a tough situation worse. One minor error that needed a tweak turned into a major issue, and the relationship between that rep and manager was damaged, all because of bad timing. The manager hadn't slowed down and emotionally unhooked, so he couldn't approach the conversation at a better time and from a better place.

Doing things at the right time fosters the right environment for change, and it also leads to building strong relationships of trust that are required for impactful coaching.

SITUATION QUESTIONS FOR REFLECTION

Now that you understand how the situation affects coaching, ask yourself the following questions:

- How do you currently create safety with your team?

- How can you tailor the environment in which you coach your team to promote their safety?

- How do you continue to build trust with your team?

MAPS SUMMARY

Coaching fails before it begins when you fail to prepare with MAPS. Coaches don't have a clear mindset, or they have the wrong attitude, or they get emotionally hooked along the way and their attitude turns bad. They don't have a plan and thus, don't coach in a smart, effective way, or they don't create a situation conducive for successful coaching. MAPS allows you to set up coaching in a way that ensures a higher success rate for reaching your coaching goals and achieving your desired outcomes.

You have numerous coaching tools to help move people from one way of doing things to another, but it doesn't matter how good the tools are if you're not properly trained and prepared to use them. Too often, leaders have a garage full of tools but lack the skillset to utilize them. Your job as a coach begins with MAPS. If you can't do the work and prepare the process beforehand, you will limit your potential, and your coaching isn't going to be successful, no matter which of the four coaching zones you apply.

MAPS only takes a few minutes. Once you get into the habit of using MAPS and practice it, the process will become second nature. Asking yourself the right questions beforehand, doing a little prep and making some good decisions will make your coaching easier and set you and your people up for great success.

NOW IT'S YOUR TURN

At this point, you should understand all the reasons for coaching, the problems, the opportunities, and the pitfalls. Hopefully, you understand the enormous power that's at your disposal.

In the next chapter, "The Coach's Playbook," we're going to dive into all four coaching zones with practical information and activities you can start using today. We'll discuss feedback, training, mentoring, and collaboration, and how and when to use them.

This is the chapter where you'll learn the specific skills and steps to becoming a master of optimized coaching. The playbook details the four coaching zones, shows you which zone is the correct one for each situation, and teaches you how to determine when it's time to switch from one coaching zone to a different one.

This isn't hard—it's easy. You're not broken and neither is your team. You're already coaching every day, and everyone needs a coach. You don't have to be a genius to coach effectively. You can do this and be great at it.

Goal and target (Focus on the solution not the problem).

Keep the goal SMART. This increases your level of success.

Assess what is missing or necessary to reach your goal.

The United States of America
SMART KASH

Goal/Target: _____

Specific, **M**easurable, **A**greed to, **R**ealistic, **T**ime Based

Knowledge: _____   Attitude: _____
Skills: _____   Habits: _____

ONE HUNDRED DOLLARS
IN GOLD COIN PAYABLE TO THE BEARER ON DEMAND

BONUS SECTION: SMART KASH

One way to ensure meaningful results from a coaching conversation is by using a tool such as SMART KASH. The concept of SMART as it relates to goal setting is discussed in Chapter 14, "The RED Zone Collaboration Process." The KASH concept adds a critical feature for dealing with barriers that can prevent the people you coach from achieving their best performance and getting top results.

Successful coaching often demands a shift in behaviors from the coachee, and having a clear target is necessary to achieve that shift. The target, or goal, is the stated intention for the coaching conversation. Ask yourself, "What do you want to accomplish with your coaching encounter?"

SMART goals accelerate results in the coaching process. They're like the afterburner on a fighter jet, thrusting the conversation, the target, and the results into a new level of acceleration.

KASH refers to the barriers that hold your coachee back from reaching their goal.

People who are being coached often jump to extremes when considering the obstacles. Expect to hear comments like, "I am not smart enough to do this," or "This will take forever to learn." The coach's job is to simplify the barrier and focus the coachee on addressing the core issue. You can do this by helping the coachee identify whether the barrier is a knowledge issue, an attitude issue, a skills issue, or a habits issue. The issue you're coaching to may encompass more than one KASH item, but in many cases, only one needs to be addressed to attain the goal.

It's critical to determine the specific issue—knowledge, attitude, skills, or habits—before determining the coaching plan. Too often, coaches jump to what appears to be obvious—but wrong—solutions for common problems.

As a corporate coach, I often saw training used as the go-to solution for team members struggling in sales or customer service. Leadership immediately assumed there was a knowledge issue, so the logical response was to provide more knowledge and skills practice. The flaw in this thinking was that these seasoned team members were spending their time learning skills they already knew. They had already demonstrated their competence with years of solid sales results.

Instead, struggling sales and customer-service people can be suffering from attitude or habits issues. If the leader, as an effective coach, had engaged in a collaboration coaching session with the team member, they would have discovered the real issue affecting the coachee's performance. Then, they could direct their efforts to the proper solution, rather than spending a lot of time and money on a solution that would never solve the problem or help them reach their goal.

Likewise, managers can write off exceptional employees, thinking they have an attitude problem because they didn't collaborate with the person and realize they had a knowledge and skills gap.

From a coaching zone perspective, knowledge and skills gaps or issues are better addressed by Zones 1, 2, and 3, while attitude and habits are best addressed with Zones 3 and 4. Although you may not be immediately aware of which of the four KASH topics is affecting the goal, you can discover it through collaboration and then adjust your coaching to the appropriate zone to remove the barrier. Also, be aware that the barrier can change over time, and leaving one unattended can cause others to emerge. For example, a team member, or an entire team, that's impaired by a knowledge issue at one point in time may suffer from an attitude issue later, especially if the knowledge issue isn't resolved. Be prepared to adjust your coaching strategy as the barriers change.

CHAPTER 17

The Coach's Playbook

The fight is won or lost far away from witnesses—behind the lines, in the gym, and out there on the road, long before I dance under those lights.

—MUHAMMAD ALI

By now, you have a firm grasp on the coaching zones. The next step is to put everything you've learned to work. Breaking the coaching code isn't just a theory but a powerful way to unlock the full potential within yourself and others.

This chapter provides a step-by-step guide based on the coaching zones and associated processes you've read about in the previous chapters. As you move through each step, take time to answer the prompts and questions fully and thoughtfully for the best results. If you need to review the zones, refer to earlier chapters as noted.

This is where the real learning begins. By applying what you've read, observing the results, and making adjustments, this is how you break the coaching code.

STEP 1: EXPLAIN THE SITUATION

You may understand the situation in your head, but to coach to it, you must document the issue and the desired result. As you move through the coaching process, refer to your responses in this section to ensure you're on track and to determine if the situation has changed. You may have to adjust your responses as you learn more about your team member, the issue, and the circumstances surrounding the situation.

- Write a complete description of the situation.

....

- Why is this topic important, and why is it especially important now?

....

- What, specifically, would you like to solve?

....

- What would be your ideal outcome?

....

STEP 2: EXPLORE YOUR MAPS

In this step, if you need to refresh your understanding of MAPS, refer to Chapter 16, "MAPS," for a detailed description of each stage: Mindset, Attitude, Plan, and Situation.

MINDSET

- What is your mindset going into the coaching?

....

- What story have you told yourself about the person or situation?

....

- What have you decided about the person(s) involved and how they will respond?

....

- How valuable do you think coaching this person can potentially be?

  ....

- What has already been decided by you or others about the outcome of this coaching?

  ....

- What have others communicated with you that is affecting the way you perceive the coachee or this matter?

  ....

- What do you need to change about your mindset that would set this situation up for greater success?

  ....

ATTITUDE

- Describe how you are feeling about coaching this situation.

  ....

- In what areas do you feel conflicted or emotionally

hooked by this situation or the relationship with the coachee?

....

- What are some potential blind spots that you may be overlooking? Think about ways you may be overexaggerating the situation or underestimating the importance of this person or issue.

....

- What fight-or-flight tendencies may exist that need to be addressed within you before having this conversation?

....

- If you are hooked or lack clarity emotionally, what steps do you need to take before having this coaching conversation? When are you going to take these steps?

....

PLAN

- What is your plan to ensure a successful coaching situation?

  ....

- What steps are you going to take?

  ....

- What resources are needed to maximize this moment?

  ....

- Who needs to be involved to increase the level of success?

  ....

SITUATION

- What safety issues need to be addressed?

  ....

- What environmental considerations need to be worked out?

  ....

- Where is the ideal location to meet?

  ....

- Who needs to be present?

  ....

- What physical barriers need to be added or removed?

  ....

- What is the current level of trust between you and the coachee?

  ....

- Have there been any trust violations that need to be addressed? What steps have you taken to address those violations or concerns?

  ....

- What distractions need to be removed before the coaching (i.e., computer, phone, messy desk, windows open/closed, door open/closed, etc.)?

  ....

- Is this the right time and moment to address this coaching situation? If not now, when would be the ideal time?

....

- What do you not know that may be hurting you and your ability to effectively coach this person and situation?

....

STEP 3: EVALUATE THE ZONES

Step 3 will guide you to the appropriate coaching zone for the situation. You may wish to refer to Chapter 3, "The New Rules of Coaching," for a summary of each of the four zones; Chapters 5 through 14 for details and examples of feedback, training, mentoring, and collaboration, and to the bonus section located at the end of Chapter 16, "MAPS," for a review of SMART KASH.

- Does the coachee have awareness of the situation?

....

- What part of KASH is affecting their awareness?

....

- Is this a knowledge issue?

  ....

- Is this an attitude concern?

  ....

- Is this a skills issue?

  ....

- Is this a habits problem?

  ....

- Did the coachee bring this topic to you?

  ....

- Are they asking you to fix their problem because they lack the ability or knowledge to address the issue(s)?

  ....

- Is this a problem they could address themselves if guided through the right questions and process?

....

- Is the coachee trying to pass off taking responsibility by bringing this to you to fix, or do they truly lack the understanding to solve this for themselves?

....

- What steps do you need to take to help them be the hero in this situation and in their own development?

....

- Do they need help processing their thoughts and feelings to help them find a solution for themselves?

....

- Which coaching zone are you going to begin with?

....

QUICK REFERENCE: AWARENESS
IN THE FOUR COACHING ZONES

Awareness is key when selecting the right coaching zone for a situation. A lack of awareness on the part of the coachee often requires starting in the lower zones, with feedback or training. As awareness and personal ownership increase, your coaching strategy may move to a higher zone, mentoring or collaboration.

- **Feedback**: The coachee lacks awareness and personal ownership. The coach needs to provide awareness of obstacles, concerns, and potential consequences. This can be a formal or informal process.

- **Training**: The coachee doesn't have the skills and knowledge to be successful. They also don't know what they don't know. The coach provides formal or informal training to create awareness and a solution to the performance barriers.

- **Mentoring**: The coachee has awareness of the performance barriers and has taken personal ownership to seek help from an expert or someone else who can provide knowledge and skills to walk through the process with them.

- **Collaboration**: The coachee has a desire and awareness to address the performance barrier, but they need help to correct their own problem. The coach fosters self-discovery and creates a deeper awareness through asking guided questions. In many cases, the coachee already has the skills and knowledge to fix their own problems. Through collaboration, they can put a viable plan in place to shift thinking, attitudes, and habits, with a new way of approaching the performance barrier.

FEEDBACK: START WITH THE SEEE MODEL

If you have identified feedback as your initial coaching stage, complete this section, which starts with the SEEE Model: Specify, Express, Explore, and Explain. You may refer to Chapter 6, "The SEEE Feedback Model," for more details. If you are beginning in a different coaching stage, skip this section and move to one of the next sections, "Training," "Mentoring," or "Collaboration."

SPECIFY: DESCRIBE THE SITUATION

- What has happened to warrant the feedback?

  ....

- What are the facts of the situation? Remember, beginning with the facts reduces conflict and defensiveness. Starting with hearsay or assumptions can start an argument.

  ....

EXPRESS: EXPLAIN HOW YOU FELT OR INTERPRETED THE SITUATION

State your view and opinion of the situation or event based on the information available to you at the time.

For example, start with the following:

- "Based on what I saw, I feel you did this..."

....

- "The way I interpreted it was this..."

....

EXPLORE ALTERNATIVES OR SUGGESTIONS

Examples of exploratory questions, instructions, and potential outcomes are as follows:

- "Help me understand the reason you said this."

....

- "What happened with following through with the customer after you received the call?"

....

- "Would you be willing to clarify your actions here?"

....

- "Next time, I would like you to do this."

....

- "If this is not corrected effectively, the consequences will be..."

....

EXPLAIN HOW THE FEEDBACK TIES TO GOALS AND SHARED PURPOSE

In this step, it is important that you express sincerity and support. Examples:

- "I know we're both committed to hitting this goal. I want to partner with you as you are growing in this role."

....

- "What else can I do to help you?"

....

Finally, if there's going to be a follow-up, establish that at the explain phase:

- "Hey, I would like us to follow up tomorrow to make sure you're feeling good with your new process."

....

TRAINING: MOR, A BETTER WAY TO TRAIN

If you have identified training as your initial coaching stage, complete this section, which starts with MOR: Motivation, Ownership, and Real-World application. You may refer to Chapter 9, "MOR: A Better Way to Train," for more details. If you are beginning in a different coaching stage, skip this section and move to one of the next sections, "Mentoring" or "Collaboration."

Start your coaching by answering these questions:

- How am I currently training?

  ....

- What's missing from my ability to become a great training coach?

  ....

- What am I doing to make sure this is a learning journey, not a learning event?

  ....

- What can I do within my role, even if I'm not an expert in the field?

  ....

Next, move through the MOR process by answering the following questions.

MOTIVATION

- What's in it for me?

  ....

- What is in this for them?

  ....

- What do I need to do to create motivation?

  ....

- What problems will this training help solve for the coachee, and how does this apply to their world?

  ....

- What type of return on their investment of time and energy can they expect to get by completing this training?

  ....

OWNERSHIP

- What do I need to own in this process?

  ....

- What do I need to do to give this person, the coachee, ownership over their learning process?

  ....

- What learning strategy would help increase their understanding and retention of the material?

  ....

- What is their learning style?

  ....

- If I don't know their learning style:

  - What graphs, charts, pictures, or other imagery can I incorporate to maximize impact for the visual learner?

    ....

  - What tools, such as stories, verbal instructions, or

discussions, can I provide to stimulate the auditory learner?

....

○ What activities and hands-on elements can I provide for the kinesthetic learner?

....

· What do I need to let go of as a training coach to allow the coachee to grow organically in the process?

....

REAL-WORLD APPLICATION

· What case studies or real-world applications can be used to increase the application and understanding of the materials?

....

· What can I do to integrate these learning processes into our real-world, day-to-day work and make sure the training is implemented?

....

MENTORING

If you have identified mentoring as your initial coaching stage, complete this section. You may refer to Chapter 10, "Introduction to Zone 3: Mentoring," for more details. If you are beginning the collaboration coaching stage, skip this section and move to the next section, "Collaboration."

One of the first steps in mentoring is creating a mentorship agreement. From Chapter 11, "Mentorship Agreements," this is a formal or informal agreement between mentor and mentee that focuses on specific issues and includes a clearly defined relationship, goal, and an action plan to achieve the goal.

Before the mentorship agreement begins, address these essential questions with your mentee:

- What expectations do you both have for the mentoring relationship?

  ....

- What format best supports these goals?

  ....

- How will you both deal with confidentiality?

  ....

- How does the mentee want to be pushed and challenged?

  ....

- What time frame will be established to work on this goal?

  ....

- What form of communication best fits both of you?

  ....

- Where and when will both parties meet? At work? Off-site? How often?

  ....

- How direct and honest does the mentee really want you to be?

  ....

- How will you both determine if the mentoring agreement was successful?

  ....

- What kind of accountability and follow-up is expected of both of you?

....

ADDRESSING THE ISSUES

- What is the perceived problem?

....

  - What is the gap? Describe the gap and identify what is missing and needs to be addressed. Remember, this is a fact-finding mission to get as much relevant information as possible to understand what is causing the problem.

  ....

  - What is the goal? As you work with the coachee, help them establish a goal statement that clearly describes where they want to end up, ultimately.

  ....

  - What is the game plan? Define the plan and steps in the process that need to take place to achieve the goal.

  ....

- If you are not a suitable candidate to mentor this person, compile a list of potential mentors: people who may provide suitable mentorship coaching.

....

- What do you need to become to effectively mentor for the coachee?

....

- What concerns need to be addressed before entering into this type of relationship?

....

POTENTIAL BARRIERS

- On a scale of one to ten, how do you rate with each of these core mentor skills:

  ○ Active listening

  ....

  ○ Building rapport

  ....

- Eye contact

....

- Effective facial expressions

....

- Tone

....

- Gestures

....

- Posture

....

- Responsive listening

....

- "I" statements

....

- Being authentic and sincere

....

- Verifying and paraphrasing

....

- What facts do you need to better understand before providing a solution or direction?

....

- What observations can you make about the coachee's world and their perspective that would affect their ability to change?

....

- What blind spots are evident in your observations?

....

- What sore spots, areas of avoidance, or forbidden topics are present in your conversations?

....

ASKING QUESTIONS

- What types of questions do you think will have the greatest effect in your discussion and will stimulate thinking?

  ....

- List at least five questions that will help guide your discussion.

  ....

- What hypothetical questions can stimulate thought about the situation?

  ....

- What questions or topics do you want to avoid that will detract from the situation?

  ....

- What stories do you think will help provide direction and guidance?

  ....

CHALLENGING THE COACHEE

- What behaviors need to be addressed with the coachee?

  ....

- What behaviors would be important for you to challenge to help bring honesty and clarity to the situation?

  ....

- Where do you need to provide feedback and awareness as the mentor in this situation?

  ....

- What training would be beneficial to help the coachee address missing skills and knowledge gaps?

  ....

MODELING

- What skills and knowledge can you, as the mentor, model that would be important for the coachee to learn?

  ....

- What behaviors and habits should you watch out for

as a mentor that could potentially hurt your mentee's credibility and integrity if modeled?

....

· How can this process help you develop your own skills and personal growth?

....

· On a scale of one to ten, rate the following items concerning your potential relationship with the coachee:

  ◦ Compatibility

  ....

  ◦ Integrity

  ....

  ◦ Expertise in this area

  ....

  ◦ Availability

  ....

- Vulnerability

....

- Personal development

....

- Motivation

....

CREATING CHANGE

- What change needs to occur for the coachee to signal this was an effective mentorship?

....

- How will you and the coachee define success?

....

- If change fails to happen, what will be your plan?

....

COLLABORATION: THE RED ZONE PROCESS

If you have identified collaboration as your initial coaching stage, complete this section. You may refer to Chapter 14, "The RED Zone Collaboration Process," for more details. Collaboration follows the RED Zone process in three stages: Reflect, Explore, and Decide.

You may wish to decide, upfront, if you are going to provide performance collaboration coaching or developmental collaboration coaching. Or, you can make that decision after the first step in the Reflect stage, Review the Results.

REFLECT
Step 1: Review the Results

If this is your first coaching session with a team member, meet with them to discuss the situation and desired outcome.

- What's our purpose in getting together?

....

- Are there metrics that are not being met?

....

- Are there behaviors holding you back from exceptional results?

  ....

- What is the perceived need?

  ....

- What are the pain points in the situation?

  ....

- What is really taking place here?

  ....

If you've had previous coaching sessions with this person, start with a review of the last session.

- How are things going?

  ....

- What successes did you experience?

  ....

- How did you celebrate your wins?

  ....

- What unforeseen barriers or obstacles did you encounter?

  ....

- How did you work through these barriers as they came up?

  ....

- How would you have done it differently?

  ....

- How have things changed since the last time we met?

  ....

- What would be relevant for us to cover, based on our last conversation?

  ....

- What are you working on now?

  ....

- How is that going?

....

Step 2A: Guide the Goal (Performance Coaching Only)

Here, the coach sets the goal. "Here is what I would like for us to talk about today."

- List the metrics and facts in the situation, avoiding generalities or opinions. This is not the time to discuss your story.

....

- Based on the facts, what story have you told yourself?

....

- What is the coachee's perception and story, considering the facts?

....

- What do you need to know and clarify, based on their comments?

....

- Verify and paraphrase their comments to ensure understanding.

....

- Do they own their results or the situation?

....

- What resistance needs to be addressed?

  ....

- Are they ready to move forward and discuss new options to address this situation?

  ....

- What has not been discussed that should be, between the coach and the coachee?

  ....

- State a single sentence goal statement for the coaching. For example: "In the next twenty minutes, I would like us to talk about how you can increase your customer satisfaction scores by ten percent in the next thirty days."

  ....

- Ensure the goal is SMART:

  ○ Is it specific?

  ....

- Is it measurable?

  ....

- Is it agreed to?

  ....

- Is it realistic?

  ....

- Is it time-based?

  ....

Step 2B: Guide the Goal (Developmental Coaching Only)

Here, the coachee sets the goal. "What would you like for us to talk about today?"

- What are the facts in the situation? Note that this question may not be relevant in the situation, depending on the goal.

  ....

- What is the coachee's perception of the situation?

  ....

- Why this topic, and why now?

  ....

- What do you need to know and clarify based on their comments?

  ....

- What potential nuggets of information is the coachee revealing?

  ....

- Verify and paraphrase their comments to ensure understanding.

  ....

- What resistance or blame needs to be addressed?

  ....

- Are they ready to move forward and discuss new options to address this situation?

....

- What has not been discussed that needs to be between the coach and the coachee?

....

- Have the coachee state in a single sentence the goal statement for the coaching. For example: "In the next twenty minutes, I would like us to talk about how I can develop my time management skills and increase my productivity each day by ten percent for the next sixty days."

....

- Ensure the goal is SMART:

    ◦ Is it specific?

    ....

    ◦ Is it measurable?

    ....

- Is it agreed to?

....

- Is it realistic?

....

- Is it time-based?

....

Step 3: Rate the Reality

- What are you currently doing to achieve this goal?

....

- What else? (Keep asking this until they empty out all their items. They will tell you when they are done.)

....

- Tell me more. (Say this for vague and generalized comments.)

....

- Once all the items have been listed, have them rate the reality. "On a scale of one to ten, with ten being the highest and one not working at all, how would you rate each of these items?"

....

- Repeat the ratings back to the coachee. Explain that anything below an eight is not effective or working.

....

- Based on these ratings, what do these results tell us about their current plan?

....

- They must acknowledge their current plan is not working before moving on to exploring options for a new plan.

....

- If their current plan has high numbers, this indicates you are probably not talking about the right topic. This may be an indication they are avoiding the real issue.

....

- Once the coachee indicates their plan is not working and they need a new plan, you can transition to the exploring stage.

....

EXPLORE: BRAINSTORMING POTENTIAL IDEAS

- If you had a magic wand, and time, money, and resources were not an issue, what would you do to solve this? (Anything goes since this is brainstorming. Start broad in your questioning and move toward more specific questions.)

....

- If you won the lottery and money was no object, what would you do?

....

- What else? (Keep asking this until they empty out all their items. They will tell you when they are done.)

....

- Tell me more. (Ask this for vague and generalized comments.)

....

- Use follow-up questions. Dig out answers to help them process potential ideas. For example, if the coachee states, "I would write a book," the coach might follow up with:

  - Where would you need to start to make that happen?

    ....

  - What steps are in that process that you could begin today?

    ....

  - Where could you go to learn more about that process and learn how to get started?

    ....

DECISION: STEPS FORWARD

Restate the brainstorming list, then ask:

- Which of these items would you like to move forward with?

  ....

- How can you make them SMART to help ensure success?

  ....

- When are you going to have that done by? The more specific their answer, the better. For example: "Friday at five p.m."

  ....

- Verify and paraphrase their comments to ensure understanding.

  ....

  ○ For example: "So it sounds like you would like to take a college class next semester, is that correct?"

    ....

  ○ Paraphrased example: "Based on what you indicated, you want to work on your personal development this year by taking a college class, reading three business journals, and working on a mentorship contract. Is that correct?"

    ....

- What resources do you need to help you to move forward?

....

- What do you need from me as the coach?

....

- When do you want to follow up on these items?

....

  - If this is performance coaching, the coach will usually decide on the follow-up time frame.

    ....

  - If this is developmental coaching, the coachee will take the lead.

    ....

PART VI CONCLUSION

There is no one way to practice perfect coaching or to become the perfect coach. Coaching is a learning process between human beings, and you will make mistakes. Don't give up.

The more you coach, the more natural these processes will become to you, and the more effective your coaching will be.

Coaching is a fluid process. If you decide to begin your coaching in Zone 1, you are not stuck in that zone, and you may come to a point where Zone 2 makes more sense for the situation. Likewise, you may begin in Zone 4 with developmental collaboration coaching, and come to a point where Zone 3, mentoring, is required. If you are self-aware, following the process of a zone, asking the right questions, and paying attention to your coachee's responses, the appropriate coaching zone will become clear to you.

As you practice your coaching skills, be aware of questions, issues, and situations that are unique to your company's industry, region, organizational structure, and culture. Take note of issues that may be specific to your department or team.

Note what works and what doesn't because this is a starting point for you and not the finish line. Over time, you will develop a playbook based on the structure you've learned in this book, but one that's unique to you, your company, and your people.

PART VI QUESTIONS FOR REFLECTION

1. Now that you have a better understanding of MAPS and coaching, go back to Chapter 2 and retake the V-Score Assessment. What has changed?

2. What excuses are you currently using that are holding you back from becoming the coach you want to be?

3. What practices are getting in the way of you experiencing dynamic growth as a coach?

4. How can you make the coaching process winnable for you personally?

Conclusion

THE BUTTERFLY EFFECT

I think it's possible for ordinary men to be extraordinary.

—ELON MUSK

The butterfly effect is a concept that states: small causes can have larger effects. The term was coined by Edward Lorenz, who derived the metaphor while researching weather patterns. He suggested that tornados in one part of the world could be influenced by minor occurrences, such as the flapping of the wings of a distant butterfly weeks earlier.

Although the metaphor can be taken to an extreme, the concept is fundamentally true. Minor changes around us can affect large shifts in our personal and professional lives. It takes just one spark to start a fire. Provided with the right environment that fire can ignite a change that spreads from one person to the next and throughout an entire organization. Leaders often fail to realize their words and actions create a spark that can light a path out of the vortex or that can set the company ablaze, engulfed in the vortex.

Gregg Levoy provides a beautiful illustration of this in his book, *Callings*. He describes the Hindu myth about god Indra: "Indra once wove a net to encompass the world, and at each knot fastened a bell. Thus, nothing could stir—not a person, not a leaf on a tree, not a single emotion—without ringing a bell, which would, in turn, set all the others to ringing."[1] The bells will ring either way, but the results will be greatly affected by how we choose to interact with the lives we touch.

My hope is that leaders will begin to explore a fresh approach to interacting with their people and getting more out of their work and their team members. Every organization is driven by their core targets and their bottom-line imperatives. I would argue how they go about achieving those targets is as important as the goals themselves. The secret to long-term growth and optimized performance is in how we manage and lead those within the team. This is why coaching is one of the most important tools in your arsenal of resources to shape change and drive efficiency. By investing a little differently into their people, leaders can increase their team's productivity, passion, and performance.

---

1   Gregg Levoy, *Callings: Finding and Following an Authentic Life* (Three Rivers: New York, 1997), 140-141.

The four zones: feedback, training, mentoring, and collaborating provide a set of tools that help the coach adapt to the needs of the moment. They meet the team member where they are at and partner with their people to move past the barriers and obstacles to experience unlimited potential.

THE REST OF JEN'S STORY

Do you remember Jen from the introduction? Years later, I ran into her again and we had a chance to catch up. She'd gone on to multiple companies where she relived the same cycle repeatedly. She would start off with short-term success, but eventually, the vortex would take her and her team hostage. She was on her second marriage, and her work continued to take a toll on her personal life. She was having the same problems, all because she had never been able to break the cycle.

As we visited, I realized there was something different about Jen. She was finally ready to move past the blame and look for a new way to approach herself and her team. When we finished talking, Jen said, "I need someone to help me see what I can't see in myself." She asked me to become her coach, and we soon began working together on her problems. In the past, she had focused on fixing everything outside of herself: her people, metrics, boss, and organization. This time was different. Jen first worked on herself, something she had avoided for many years. She became aware of some destructive patterns that were hurting her relationships. As she worked on new skills, her relationships changed, and her team responded to her direction in a healthy way. Her marriage began to heal, and she and her husband became the friends and marriage partners they always wanted to be. She became an engaged parent, especially at a time when her kids needed her the most. As Jen got stronger as a leader, her metrics and performance followed. She was eventually offered that elusive promotion she always wanted and thought she needed to be a success. However, when it finally came, she turned the promotion down. Jen realized she wanted to spend more time on things that mattered most in her life: her personal development, her family, and her team, whom she had begun to care deeply about. For the first time in her career, Jen was truly free.

THE WRITING ON THE WALL

In the introduction, we noted that the first step to moving past the vortex is acknowledging the problem. Jen's transformation happened when she stopped clinging to the image of herself and her career that she had created and took an honest look at the reality of her situation. For many leaders, this is the most difficult step toward adopting a coaching culture.

When a vortex permeates a company's culture, significant issues can become hidden, lost in the day-to-day activity of the business. This vortex creates a disparity between a company's image of itself and the reality experienced by employees, but you must be willing to open your eyes to the truth of your company to move forward.

I saw an example of this when I was consulting for a large real estate management corporation. As I entered the main floor of the building, the first thing I noticed was the writing on the wall: the company's mission and vision statements, core values, and company pillars were plastered all over the walls above the workers' cubicles. I caught a glimpse of coffee mugs and literature on desks that reinforced these same messages. I made my way to the conference room where I was meeting the leaders of the company, and we all settled in around the big table.

"Can I ask you all a question?" I said.

"Sure, what is it?" one replied.

"What are you compensating for?"

They looked at me and looked around at each other. "What do you mean?" they wanted to know.

"Well, the mission and the mantras and all the writing on the walls. Does this reflect your current culture, or are you attempting to get everyone on board by showcasing it on the walls?"

The men around the table laughed, but it did not take long before I had my answer.

The messages on the walls reflected who they wanted to be, or more accurately, who they thought they should be. Unfortunately, their true culture was far from the corporate rhetoric and clichés that had been determined by a few select committee members in a boardroom. They were using marketing tools to try to sell it since they could not authentically create it.

This tactic reminds me of children who sleep with their history books under their pillow hoping—perhaps through osmosis—all the information will magically flood into their minds overnight. What child does not dream of a quick shortcut to their education process to avoid the tedious work required to be academically successful? We laugh at children who come up with such implausible ideas, yet when similar hope strategies appear in the corporate culture, we blindly embrace them. But behind the writing on the walls and company mantras chanted at weekly meetings comes the stark reality that the only people these folks—those who perpetrate this imaginary culture—are fooling, are themselves.

START NOW

If you don't take steps to break the coaching code today, you risk looking back years from now with regret. Don't waste anymore time. No matter where you are, you can start transforming your work, your relationships, and ultimately your results, today—right this minute.

As you put into practice what you've learned and approach zone optimization, you'll see the corporate vortex diminish. Your organization will reap the benefits of better people, performance, and results—all the things leaders want and highly effective companies have. These things happen when you develop a coaching culture.

The first step is looking at yourself. Then, begin to assess your team. Take small steps to begin integrating zone coaching into your culture. Use the forms and tools provided in the Coach's Playbook to help you get started. Go to BreakingTheCoachingCode.com for more resources, blogs, and other tools to support you through the transition. My team will work with you to integrate these new practices within your team and ultimately your organization's culture.

DON'T GIVE UP

I said at the beginning, "Coaching is easy," but as I also indicated, it's just as easy to not coach. There will always be competing priorities and fire drills that will edge out your proactive focus. It's easy to blame others, punish people, or simply ignore performance issues, but if this approach had been serving you well, I doubt that you would have picked up this book. It's just as easy to start coaching.

The zone coaching steps and habits need practice to be effective. You will fail at times and become frustrated, especially when you do not see immediate success. Don't give up. Breakthroughs will happen if you keep working on the steps. And if you think you know everything about coaching but you have never seen results and don't think it's worth the effort, remember this final story about my son.

When my oldest son was about six years old, my wife and I tried to get him involved in taking music lessons. We would let him choose any instrument, but since we'd noticed him tinkering around on the piano, we asked him how he felt about piano lessons. He looked at us and said, "I already know how to play the piano." I was perplexed by his comment. What did he mean? He went on to tell us that a friend of his had shown him how to play a single song, so now he knew how to play and didn't need to take lessons. I tried to explain that knowing how to play a song is very different than learning an instrument, reading music, and mastering skills. As silly as this sounds, it's not so different than what I've witnessed in many companies over the years. Leaders make similar assumptions about their mastery of coaching, thinking that just because they've tried to do it, dabbled in it, and tinkered around with it, they already know all about coaching.

There is a substantial difference between taking a class, reading a book, or learning a single lesson, and mastering the art of coaching, which comes with practice. And just as my son, with practice, could learn to play the piano, you can learn coaching. In fact, you have it in you to become a masterful coach.

JOIN THE REVOLUTION

Besides the obvious financial benefits of coaching, more importantly, there is another reason to take steps toward creating a coaching culture. All around the world, there is a new and exciting revolution taking place in organizations. Companies are seeing how their people make a difference in creating industry innovations, increasing cost efficiencies, and developing talent and growth from the inside out. Companies aren't buying their all-stars; they are developing them, at a fraction of the cost of recruiting and hiring superior, external talent. These revolutionary companies are reducing turnover and increasing engagement. They aren't merely trying to get more work from their people; they are creating loyal champions who believe in the mission and direction of the organization. The mission is not a plaque on the wall. It's written on the hearts and minds of the people.

Come join the revolution! Coaching doesn't have to be an esoteric, difficult-to-understand concept. It doesn't need to be some checklist the legal department makes leaders follow to protect the company from lawsuits. It can be transformative and empowering. You now have the tools to begin breaking the coaching code. Use them to unlock the potential within your team. Open the door and see what results await you and your people on the other side.

Acknowledgments

There are many leadership and management topics that I have studied over the years. However, none of them have made a greater impact to my personal and professional growth more than coaching. Although coaching has systems and methods to guide the process, the heart of coaching is about understanding ourselves and others. Along the way, I have been exposed to many coaching books and programs that have helped shape my understanding of the principles and practices, but my greatest understanding came through watching the coaches who inspired my life personally. They not only taught critical principles, they lived them in a real and authentic way. For the longest time, I thought coaching was only a process; however, I learned from these amazing coaches that it is actually a lifestyle.

I want to acknowledge these special individuals who have inspired my life and coaching journey.

Robert Morris was my fifth-grade teacher. He taught me the power of investing in people. His openness to seeing the potential in others helped me see the potential in myself. He never had the title of coach, but his life was committed to bringing out the brilliance in others.

Dr. Woody Northcutt inspired every life he touched. He was my beloved college professor that spent countless hours listening and guiding me through some of my toughest personal and professional questions. He never pushed his agenda or answers on me, even when I begged for a quick answer to my problems. He helped me find the answers within myself. In a world full of opinions and voices competing to tell us how we should think and live, he was a person that taught me how to listen to the most important voice, the voice within. Woody, I miss you dearly.

Dr. Shohreh Aftahi taught me the value of seeing the best in people. She never gave up on anyone. Even when they failed, she was right there to help them back up and grow through the experience. She helped me to stop seeing people through my judgments and empower others with the freedom to change. There are few people I have met who have inspired so many lives and shaped people from the inside out as she has with her life and career.

James Thacker is a mentor and friend. He taught me the power of asking better questions. If you ask the wrong questions, you inevitably will get the wrong answers. He had a way of changing my entire view of a situation by simply changing the question.

When I first started coaching, it was not a natural skill. I had a certification, a new process, and some scripted questions to get me started, but I lacked the deeper understanding that can only come through practice and experience. David Whitaker allowed me to partner with his team and himself early on as a coach. He gave me the gift that few leaders would have ever given any new coach, the ability to fail. He believed in me and my skills when I didn't even believe in myself at times. Through his patience, guidance, and friendship, I grew as a coach and as a person.

London, Eowyn, and Gavin are my three children. They continue daily to shape my understanding of coaching. They help keep the main thing the main thing. With such authenticity and simplicity, they help me keep the world in perspective when I try to overcomplicate things. When I get in the way of myself and my own growth, I watch them and realize what is truly important. I know it sounds odd, but in so many ways, my children are my heroes. By the end, I will have learned so much more from them than I probably ever taught them.

Jose Luis Sifuentes is a friend and mentor. For years, he has modeled what optimized coaching is about. He offers sound feedback when I need to hear it. He is one of the most gifted trainers and facilitators I know, and he continues to help me grow in the art. He has been a mentor and a guide when I step out to try new things. There are few friends that come along that provide such a depth of wisdom, trust, and fun. Jose Luis is a rare friend and coach who has changed my life.

Over the course of writing this book, Susan Paul has partnered with me to coach me through the process. She has helped guide me to understand how to take my thoughts and ideas and put them into a form that I hope inspires others. I appreciate her wisdom and patience to help me. She is not only an author I admire; I have the honor to call her my friend.

Finally, my sincere gratitude to Karina Branson from ConverSketch. Her illustrations helped enhance the book in a wonderful way.

About the Author

DAVID ADUDDELL is an international speaker, business coach, and senior leadership development consultant based in Denver, Colorado. Over the last two decades, he has partnered with Fortune 500 companies across diverse industries, including telecom, insurance, automotive, healthcare, education, and public sector. He specializes in integrating blended and innovative solutions that focus on increasing productivity and performance. His tailored and inside-out approach helps organizations reduce time away from the job and maximize learning moments.

David has a Master of Business Administration degree with a specialization in Leadership Development. He is also a trained executive and business coach. He began his career as a professor teaching at a university outside of Denver. He would later move into the corporate world as an executive coach and leadership facilitator for one of the big four telecom companies. He then put his knowledge to the test by taking a senior manager role in which he managed multimillion-dollar budgets and hundreds of team members in regions across the US. His team went on to be in the top three markets for the entire organization. This provided him firsthand knowledge of how to take time-tested leadership principles and apply them in real-world situations. Eventually, he would return to his passion of learning and development by starting his own company, where he would help other organizations build unique learning solutions to improve performance.

As a senior leadership consultant with Zoe Training, David has years of experience delivering core content in a fun and meaningful way. He believes long-term change happens with a tailored approach to solutions. From going deeper in assessing core gaps to a blended approach in creating a cultural transformation, his practical and fresh approach meets your team where they are. His passion is to help teams get from where they are to where they want to go.

David and his wife, Stephanie, have three children and live in Parker, Colorado. He and his family spend time hiking fourteeners (mountains with a peak of 14,000 feet in elevation) and enjoy traveling together. This is his first book.

If you would like to learn more, go to Zoetraining.com. You can contact David Aduddell directly at David@zoetraining.com.

www.ingramcontent.com/pod-product-compliance
Lightning Source LLC
Chambersburg PA
CBHW022051210326
41519CB00054B/303